Professional Services Marketing

The Marketing Series is one of the most comprehensive collections of books in marketing and sales available from the UK today.

Published by Butterworth-Heinemann on behalf of the Chartered Institute of Marketing, the series is divided into three distinct groups: *Student* (fulfilling the needs of those taking the Institute's certificate and diploma qualifications; *Professional Development* (for those on formal or self-study vocational training programmes); and *Practitioner* (presented in a more informal, motivating and highly practical manner for the busy marketer).

Formed in 1911, the Chartered Institute of Marketing is now the largest professional marketing management body in Europe with over 22,000 members and 25,000 students located worldwide. Its primary objectives are focused on the development of awareness and understanding of marketing throughout UK industry and commerce and in the raising of standards of professionalism in the education, training and practice of this key business discipline.

Books in the series

How to Sell a Service
Malcolm H. B. McDonald
International Marketing Digest
Edited by Malcolm H. B. McDonald and S. Tamer Cavusgil
Managing Your Marketing Career
Andrew Crofts
The Marketer's Dictionary
Norman A. Hart and John Stapleton
The Marketing Book
Edited by Michael J. Baker
The Marketing Digest
Edited by Michael J. Thomas and Norman E. Waite
Marketing Plans: how to prepare them, how to use them
Malcolm H. B. McDonald
Marketing Research for Managers
Sunny Crouch
Marketing to the Retail Trade
Geoffrey Randall
The Marketing of Services
Donald Cowell
The Practice of Advertising
Edited by Norman A. Hart and James O'Connor
The Practice of Public Relations
Edited by Wilfred Howard
The Principles and Practice of Export Marketing
E. P. Hibbert
Professional Services Marketing
Neil Morgan
Relationship Marketing: integrating quality, customer service and marketing
Martin Christopher, Adrian Payne and David Ballantyne
Solving the Management Case
Angela Hatton, Paul Roberts and Mike Worsam
The Strategy of Distribution Management
Martin Christopher

Professional Services Marketing

Neil Morgan

Published in association with the Chartered Institute of Marketing

Butterworth-Heinemann Ltd
Linacre House, Jordan Hill, Oxford OX2 8DP

🌼   PART OF REED INTERNATIONAL BOOKS

OXFORD   LONDON   BOSTON
MUNICH   NEW DELHI   SINGAPORE   SYDNEY
TOKYO   TORONTO   WELLINGTON

First published 1991

British Library Cataloguing in Publication Data
Morgan, Neil
    Professional services marketing.
    I. Title
    658.8

ISBN 0 7506 0090 X

Photoset by Deltatype Ltd, Ellesmere Port, Cheshire
Printed and bound in Great Britain by
Billings & Sons Ltd, Worcester

12/06/92

Contents

Preface

The original idea for this book on professional services marketing actually had very little to do with my idea of how best to spend a year of my working life. I was driven to produce the book in the face of the overwhelming demand from individual professionals, firms, and even professional bodies, for a comprehensive source of information, frameworks and ideas in the areas of marketing and strategy. Having sent out literally hundreds and hundreds of copies of articles and papers that I had written on various aspects of this area, and spent many hundreds of hours in meetings and on the telephone talking to professionals and marketers seeking information and advice, it became obvious that unless I made available a comprehensive text of this nature then I could probably write off the next three years of my life reacting to enquiries from professionals.

This book is, therefore, first and foremost a reaction to the almost insatiable demand for knowledge and information about the subjects of marketing and strategy from working professionals and professional service firms.

This obviously presents a number of problems. The biggest of these is a need to balance the approach taken to ensure that the book is sufficiently accessible to the professional while maintaining the depth necessary to present the available academic, theoretical and conceptual developments and frameworks needed for a full and complete understanding of the issues of marketing and strategy. Walking this tightrope is obviously potentially dangerous and it may well be that in some chapters the book falls off this narrow path in either direction. However, reviews of the draft manuscript by a large number of professionals suggest that the book generally achieves this balancing act successfully.

While this book obviously represents a good deal of thought, analysis, reading, cumulative experience and general hard work on my part, the whole process has been greatly helped by a number of people.

First, a debt of gratitude must be acknowledged to my primary research collaborator, colleague and friend Professor Nigel Piercy. Nigel's ideas, approach and academic work have greatly shaped my whole approach to the area of marketing and strategy and his advice upon specific issues and problems has been invaluable. At Cardiff my research assistant, Rob Morgan, has also assisted greatly in the collection of the available material and provided a sounding board for many of my ideas.

A rather different debt is owed to a large number of individuals and professional service firms with whom I have been fortunate enough to share ideas, information and experiences and to those firms with which I have gained invaluable insight through consultancy work over the past three years. Many individuals have contributed to discussion in this book and some have provided even more practical help by reading various drafts of the manuscript. Those individuals who have stimulated my thoughts in particular include: Robert Pay at Clifford Chance; Chris Stoakes of Stephenson Harwood; Steven Clues at Richard Ellis; James Mendelssohn at Neville Russell; Steve Blundell at Touche Ross; Joe Wang at Building Design Partnership; Robert Morris at Ellis and Buckle; Nick Charman at Cooper Lancaster; Chris Bunting at D.J. Freeman; Chris Arnold at Richards Butler; Steven Sidkin at Fox Williams and all of those involved in the Professional Services Marketing Group.

The physical process of developing the book was created and implemented by a number of dedicated, flexible and, above all, unbelievably tolerant administrative staff at the Cardiff Business School. Kath Hollister typed and produced the majority of the chapters, Sally Jarratt typed a number of chapters and worked long into the evenings and weekends to produce figures and illustrations, make corrections and put the whole thing together. Other chapters were typed very ably and quickly by Nowel Chan and Karen Trigg. Without the support of these people this book would still exist only in the farthest reaches of my mind.

Last, but certainly not least, a rather different debt is owed to my partner Catherine, who displayed remarkable tolerance and under-standing in the face of my almost maniacal obsession with producing this book. For the hours, evenings, weekends and weeks that she gave up I shall remain eternally grateful.

This is not an academic textbook in the traditional sense at all. It does synthesize existing academic research undertaken by myself and academic colleagues all over the world. This is, however, combined with consultancy experience and is designed to cater for the needs of individual professionals and professional service firms rather than academics and students. While many people have contributed both directly and indirectly to the development and content of the book any failings or shortcomings are naturally wholly the responsibility of the author.

Neil Morgan

Part One
Marketing and the
Professions

The whole area of professional services marketing has exploded into the world of most of the professions in the past decade. What had previously been viewed as something of a 'taboo' issue in many professions is now exciting a great deal of interest from individual professionals, professional service firms and even professional bodies in most professions. This book is a response to professionals' demand and seemingly insatiable appetite for any material, research, knowledge and expertise on the subject of professional services marketing.

This growth in the interest of marketing is very obviously not an altruistic and cerebral development on the part of most professionals. It is largely a result of the increasing competition that professional service firms of all kinds are experiencing in the marketplaces they serve. The changing competitive nature of professional service markets has been driven by three key developments in the past decade:

1   The relaxation of regulations concerning promotion and allied business development activities in a large number of professions.
2   Increasing client sophistication in many professional marketplaces leading to demands for more innovative and complex professional services, a greater emphasis upon client service and pressure upon professional service margins.
3   The business environment in which most professional service firms operate has become not only more complex, but is changing with increasing rapidity in terms of deregulation, diffusion of technology, economic volatility, demographic change, globalization, etc.

The response of many professionals, and professional service firms, to this new competitive environment has been to look towards marketing as some sort of potential panacea to these problems. This first section focuses upon exactly what marketing is, its role in professional services and how professional service firms have tended to respond to, and utilize, marketing as a part of the management and strategic development of their businesses.

1 Introduction to marketing

Marketing is not often viewed as a 'neutral' term in the context of professional service businesses. Indeed, within the professions in general, marketing is probably the management function that causes professionals more problems than any other. Marketing continues to provoke emotional debate revealing a wealth of preconceived ideas which rapidly become entrenched in large numbers of professional service firms of all types.

Fully qualified professionals have something of a problem in that they are, almost by definition, experts. They are not however, by and large, experts in marketing. A failure on the part of many professionals to recognize this has led to widespread misconceptions about what marketing actually is, what it entails and the role that it has to play in the management and development of professional service firms. Left unchallenged these misconceptions and preconceived ideas can, and do, form substantial and intractable barriers to the development of marketing within professional service firms.

In the practical setting it is particularly useful to confront these preconceived ideas and misconceptions and make them explicit as early as possible. This can expose the source of many existing and potential problems with the marketing development of a firm and help to solve them by 'neutralizing' marketing as a management issue. There exists within many professions a whole mythology of marketing that has been a contributory factor in the difficulty that many firms have and are facing in confronting the marketing issue. Before moving on to clarify what marketing actually is then it can be very useful to confront and de-bunk the myths.

The 'myths' of marketing

Marketing is advertising and selling

There is widespread belief at partner-level within most professions that marketing is, in essence, the combination of the activities of advertising and selling. This is largely a reflection of the typology of marketing that exists in the minds of many consumers who base their ideas upon the most visible of marketing communications activities. Who of us are not constantly bombarded by brash television commercials, ever increasing volumes of 'junk mail' and calls from telesales agencies? While it is perfectly understandable that average consumers might base their perception of marketing upon the most tangible and highly visible forms of marketing communications, one might have hoped that professionals running professional service businesses would be less inclined to confuse such misconceptions with the reality of marketing.

While advertising and personal selling are both legitimate marketing communications activities they represent only a very limited section of the whole marketing function.

Our firm doesn't 'do' any marketing

Often found in conjunction with our first 'myth' is the belief that if a firm does not employ specialist marketers either in-house or as consultants, or does not print glossy brochures and advertise, then it does not 'do' any marketing. From a practical point of view any firm that has not attracted, or cannot attract, some clients who have needs that can be met by the expertise and skills of that particular firm will be out of business in a short time. Any firm that exists for more than a few months is *ipso facto* 'doing' marketing – even if it is implicitly and at a very rudimentary level. I have also yet to come across a firm that, at the very least, fails to have a logo on its headed paper and a small information leaflet about what the firm does.

All professional service firms are involved in marketing their services whether or not they realize it explicitly. The critical point that needs to be made to those firms that believe this myth is that once they have accepted that they are implicitly involved in marketing, it may be more effective to make their marketing activities explicit in order that they be properly planned, resourced, co-ordinated and evaluated.

Our marketing partner 'does' our marketing

Many professional service firms are now sufficiently 'advanced' in their perceptions of the marketing issue that they assign responsibility for the marketing function within the firm to an individual partner. In many cases this is nothing more than an attempt on the part of the executive or management committee to make the 'problem' of marketing go away by giving it to a specific individual. In many firms the role of marketing partner is still seen as the 'short straw' and in a number of firms this is an area of responsibility given to the newest and most junior member of the partnership. In one firm that I have worked with the marketing partner confessed that she became responsible for marketing simply because she was the only partner to miss the partners' meeting that was discussing the issue and was therefore unable to 'wriggle out' of it! Firms in which this myth predominates usually have partners who have little idea about what marketing as a management function actually entails and would prefer to keep it that way. Even firms which are relatively 'enlightened' in marketing terms often have large numbers of partners who believe this myth – try asking some of your partners about the firm's approach to marketing! In such firms there is little or no recognition that *all* client contact and service provision staff are involved in the firm's marketing efforts.

Marketing orientation means meeting client needs at any cost

This myth often exists amongst partners and staff who have heard a bit about marketing. This is the extreme form of the economic argument against the marketing of professional services. This argument runs along the lines 'marketing means giving clients exactly what they want – and they all want superior service for very low fees which means that we go out of business'. This myth is also perpetuated by those few individuals who go on short courses about marketing and become immediate marketing 'evangelists', planning extensive, sophisticated marketing strategies with little or no thought for the profit and growth goals of the firm. Such evangelists can actually damage the introduction of marketing in a professional firm by fuelling this myth amongst other partners.

So what exactly is marketing?

While there are a large number of 'official' definitions of marketing developed by professional bodies in various parts of the world, many do not actually help to increase our understanding of the role of marketing in the professional service context. For example, the Chartered Institute of Marketing definition is:

> Marketing is the management process responsible for identifying, anticipating and satisfying customer requirements profitably.

While from an academic viewpoint there is actually little that can be considered controversial or inaccurate in this definition, in the present context such a definition fails to answer convincingly the question that partners most often pose, 'So what is marketing all about?' In this context a far more useful and potentially illuminating definition of marketing may be:

> Marketing is the management skill of matching the firm's personnel, resources and expertise with client needs in such a way that the firm achieves its long-term goals and the client receives continued satisfaction.

While this personal definition of marketing as it applies to the professional service context is relatively long-winded when compared to most 'official' definitions, it does seem to help partners and staff in professional service firms gain a much greater insight into the role and objectives of marketing.

The marketing function

While the above definition of marketing is useful and to a certain extent informative, many professionals remain concerned about the true nature of marketing as a function until the marketing process is broken down into a number of discreet, tangible, more easily identified tasks and activities. Such a list for professional services marketing could be at least as long as this book. However, a number of the key activities that are central to any professional services marketing function are:

- Researching and analysing the existing marketplaces for the firm's service offerings.
- Identifying coherent segments in the marketplace that exhibit relatively similar needs.
- Analysing the firm's resources, personnel and areas of expertise.
- Designing service offerings which translate internal strengths into specific services that meet the needs of particular segments.
- Offering only those services and targetting only those market segments that enable the firm to achieve its long-term objectives.
- Communicating the service offerings to existing and potential clients.
- Measuring client satisfaction with services and using this information within the firm.

In general terms these marketing activities add up to three major roles for marketing:

1 To ensure that current clients remain clients of the firm.
2 To generate more business from the existing client base.
3 To attract new clients to use the firm's services.

While by no means exhaustive these activities will form the basis of any professional services marketing programme. Having identified a number of key marketing tasks and activities however, there does appear to be an assumption on the part of some professionals and a lot of consultants and academics that all these activities need to be carried out by one individual or a separate functional department. While this may in fact be appropriate for a number of professional service firms it is certainly not a necessity and may even be positively damaging in a large number of professional service firms. You do not have to install a marketing manager or department in order to successfully introduce a marketing function into your firm.

In this sense the process view of marketing can be useful in demonstrating a larger view of the role of marketing in service businesses. The earlier definition of marketing talked about a 'management skill of matching'. It is important to note that 'management' in this context means just that – anyone and everyone involved in the management of the firm. This is not just a skill and set of activities for which the marketing partner and/or manager needs to be responsible.

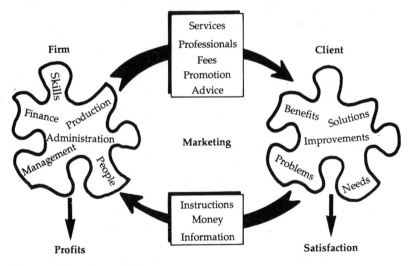

Figure 1.1 *The matching process*

The process of marketing can therefore be viewed as the matching of all of the internal elements of a firm with the external needs and problem solutions desired by clients in the marketplace. This model of marketing (Figure 1.1) also has a very realistic edge. If you look closely at the two pieces of the puzzle you will see that there is no perfect fit between them – they match up very roughly but not perfectly. A colleague pointed out that when his four-year-old son was presented with a similar problem he solved it quite simply and effectively by putting the two pieces together as best he could and then bashing them with a blunt instrument until the match was made and the pieces hung together. This image of marketing as a blunt instrument which forces some degree of matching between the firm and its markets has a good deal of validity in my experience of professional services marketing.

Marketing as a philosophy

Marketing can, and has, also been viewed as more than just a function and a process. It can also be seen at one level to be a business philosophy – a way of organizing and running a business. This is commonly known as the marketing concept. In its crudest terms the marketing concept in this context is built around a notion that 'the client is king'. Thus the marketing concept holds that everything that an organization is and does is only important in terms of the way that it impacts upon existing and potential clients in the marketplace. Therefore, a professional service firm that has adopted the marketing concept will organize itself around the central issue of satisfying client needs. While one may have some intuitive sympathy with the logic behind this concept it can be off-putting to unenlightened partners in professional service firms. If this is potentially the case in your firm introduce them to marketing functions and activities first and let them work their own way up to a recognition and acceptance of the marketing concept.

There are, therefore, a number of ways in which to view marketing – each of them equally valid and complementary. However, when we come to look at marketing in the professional service context specifically, it is obvious that there are a number of characteristics of services in general that impinge significantly upon how we market professional services. It is worth considering these characteristics of services here in the introductory chapter since reference will be made to the problems and opportunities caused by these characteristics repeatedly throughout the book. In the conceptual and academic study of services marketing the most commonly mentioned characteristics of services, which are primarily the characteristics that also differentiate services from products, are:

- intangibility
- inseparability
- heterogeneity
- perishability.

8

Intangibility

All services are characterized by a degree of intangibility. Professional services are usually seen to be more intangible than most other types of services. This is obviously a vital characteristic for professional service marketers since, unlike tangible goods, with professional services it is often impossible for potential clients to pre-test a service as a part of his or her purchase decision-making process. While marketers of goods can invite consumers to taste, feel, smell, hear and physically test most products, the intangibility characteristic does not afford this luxury to marketers of professional services.

Intangibility is obviously not an absolute term. It would be difficult to think of any service that was purely intangible and had no tangible elements associated with it. Most services, as with most goods, can be viewed as a mix of tangible and intangible offerings to the buyer. Even within the professional service context (Figure 1.2) one can view varying degrees of intangibility both between professions and within the service offerings of one profession. We can therefore view intangibility as a relative continuum in the professional service context.

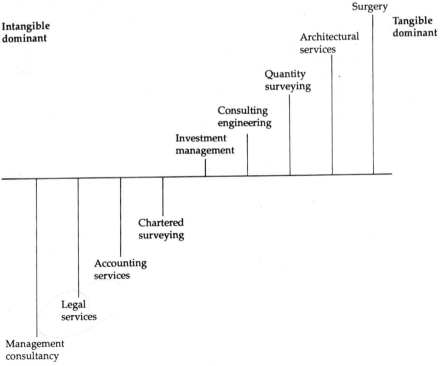

Figure 1.2 *Degrees of intangibility*

Inseparability

Inseparability in this marketing sense refers to the ability to separate the service received by the client from the person of the professional providing the service. This means that the service is often consumed, at least partially, at the same time that it is provided. For example, in litigation much of the service provided to the client is consumed as it is produced in the courtroom. It is also difficult to separate the professional providing the service from the service itself in this example. The quality of the legal litigation service provided is largely inseparable from the professional skill of the individual lawyer.

A further consideration of inseparability will reveal that in a number of professional services the client actually takes part in the production process. For example, a physician cannot produce a physical medical examination without the patient being present at some point. Similarly an accountancy firm could not undertake an audit without the involvement of the staff of the client organization.

Heterogeneity

Since the provision of service in most professions is largely inseparable from the person of the professional service provider it follows that standardization of service is almost impossible as individuals differ in personality, skill, knowledge, communications, etc. Although some professional services can be routinized to a certain degree, e.g. conveyancing for residential property, most professional services are almost completely 'customized' and will be different every time that professional service is performed. This means that achieving a standardized professional service offering to clients is impossible in most types of professional service firm. Thus quality control is a central problem for firms caused by the heterogeneous nature of professional services. This can also cause problems for clients and potential clients who find it almost impossible to make rational quality judgements before they experience the professional service from a particular firm.

Perishability

The vast majority of professional services are perishable in nature, i.e. they cannot be stored and used at some future time when demand occurs. In a management consultancy firm when there are no assignments in hand the professional service capability of the consultants is lost. It cannot be performed and stored for some future

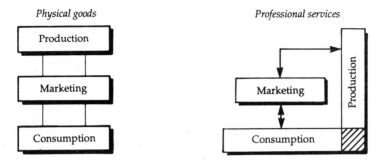

Figure 1.3

client. This characteristic perishability causes many problems for many professional service firms. Most firms suffer from fluctuations in demand since services cannot be performed and stored during slack periods in anticipation of future demand thus firms often have problems trying to cope with demand peaks. While firms can sometimes overcome some of these problems with individual services by hiring additional staff on a temporary basis, sub-contracting some work to other firms, or in the case of audit services, persuading clients to change their year ends, this characteristic causes problems for many professional service firms.

Objectives of the book

This book is not designed to be an all-encompassing definitive piece of academic work. It is planned to be a useful book that is referred to frequently in the office rather than an esoteric tome of wisdom. There are areas that this book does not cover – pricing and service development being the two most obvious areas. The contents and structure of the book reflect the areas in which my academic research and professional consultancy experiences have revealed that partners and professional service marketers experience problems and exhibit disquiet and uncertainty. If the approach taken in the rest of the book is a little unconventional in academic terms this is as a result of the focus being upon the areas of most need from the professionals' point of view. As a marketing academic this of course can be viewed as a 'market orientation' in my writing – analyse the market, identify needs and use my knowledge and experience to design and write a book to fulfil those needs. That is my story and I intend to stick to it!

This book differs in its approach to the other books in this field. Again as a marketing man I can claim this to be a simple strategic decision based upon the need for competitive differentiation. However, the difference is actually more fundamental than that. This book, unlike its rivals, does not merely take marketing theories and concepts from what we know about the marketing of products and some types of services and translate this into the professional service context. The book is deliberately titled *Professional Services Marketing* not marketing professional services. The professional service context is a peculiar one. It deserves a book about the peculiarities, irrationalities and idiosyncracies of professional services marketing as a unique and different type of marketing rather than simply writing about the areas in which marketing is similar in the professional service context to other types of marketing. While some might claim that this is merely 'splitting hairs' it does have a significant impact upon the approach and content of this book which I believe will be recognized and valued by most of the readers.

2 Marketing in professional service firms

It will be argued throughout this book that there are a number of features of most professions which make the professional service context different from other types of businesses. It is for this reason that this book is specifically centred upon 'professional services marketing' as distinct from simply trying to market professional services. Some of these differences will be highlighted here by way of an examination of some of the existing problems faced by both professional service firms attempting to develop a marketing function and those responsible for marketing within professional service firms.

Marketing and professional ethics

The age-old argument concerning the ethics of marketing within professions is beginning to die of natural causes but still remains a contentious issue in some firms and even some professions, e.g. medicine. Most of the arguments surrounding this debate are caused by a form of the 'myths about marketing' problem discussed in Chapter 1. Most of the 'anti-marketing' arguments are actually anti-advertising arguments. Some of the problems concerning the confusion of many professions over the difference between advertising and marketing were fuelled by the professional bodies themselves. This was certainly true of the accountancy and legal professions who presented their relaxation of professional guidelines upon forms of advertising and marketing communications as allowing professionals to undertake 'marketing'. It is unsurprising that many professionals are confused over the difference between marketing and advertising since, at least in 1979 and 1984, the ICAEW and Law Society seem to have been similarly confused. (Many marketers within these professions would argue that this confusion exists even today.)

This book is not the medium for an in-depth analysis of the arguments that have been proposed in the debate over advertising and the professions. For those who are particularly interested in this area an excellent article has been written by David Stafford (1988).[1]

Once the debate in this area is widened to examine the role of marketing within the professions and the ethical issue then the arguments become relatively straightforward. I would argue that for a number of reasons the traditional argument that marketing is inconsistent with professional ethics should be turned on its head. Any professional firm that isn't actively seeking to develop its marketing should be subject to disciplinary action from the relevant professional body. While this perspective may seem to be somewhat radical there are a number of underlying arguments to back up such an 'extreme' view:

1   Marketing is a sign of competition between firms within a profession – very few firms begin marketing development unless forced to consider the issue by the competitive nature of the marketplace. Competition is almost always good for clients, particularly in sectors where competition has historically been somewhat limited.

2   Marketing is by its very nature concerned with satisfying the needs of clients. Any move away from the professional 'production orientation' towards a marketing orientation has to be good for clients and good for the reputation and image of professions.

3   Marketing communications can give potential clients a far better basis for choosing between firms. A better-informed choice is much more likely to result in a mutually beneficial firm–client relationship. As we shall see later in Chapter 9 marketing communications in the professional service context has a strong educational role for clients.

4   A market orientation within a firm usually leads to a client perceiving a higher quality service. As we shall discover in Chapter 12 there is a strong relationship between marketing and quality in the professional service context which can be managed to produce client perceptions of higher quality. This is obviously beneficial to both firm and client.

Thankfully this argument appears to be being 'won' in marketing's favour in most medium and large professional service firms in a large number of professions. It will doubtless raise its head within the medical profession in the early 1990s and is still an issue in a number of smaller firms in professions of all types. I suspect, however, that the acceptance of marketing to date has been based more upon a 'new realism' in terms of competitive environment than upon the types of argument set forth above. Although I would argue against 'looking such a gift horse in the mouth', unless this issue is settled and won by informed logical argument rather than grudging and perhaps temporary acceptance, then the issues associated with the argument of marketing and ethics will continue to provide internal barriers to the potential marketing development of the firm.

The present role and status of marketing

This book was conceived and designed as a result of some empirical research projects that I undertook at the Cardiff Business School. These research projects were designed to determine the reality of the role and status of marketing *within* firms in a number of professions. The limited academic research undertaken in professional services marketing at the time of writing this book offered little to professional service marketers for a number of fairly obvious reasons:

- Most of the existing literature emanated from the USA and is seen by most professionals as difficult to translate into physical actions outside of the US.
- Empirical research by academics has been particularly scarce. The limited amount of empirical work that has been undertaken has focused upon advertising (Shimp and Dyer, 1978; Smith and Meyer, 1980; Upah and Uhr, 1981; Traynor, 1983; Carver and King, 1984)[2] in the USA and to a lesser extent in the UK (Watkins and Wright, 1985; Hind, 1986; Diamantopoulos *et al*, 1987).[3] To a more limited extent some empirical work has focused upon consumer and organizational buying behaviour, particularly in terms of factors influencing the selection of professional service firms (George and Solomon, 1980; Hughes and Kasulis, 1985; Lynn, 1987).[4]
- Most of the problems with marketing development that I have encountered through consultancy experience and interviews with professional service marketers relate to *internal* barriers to marketing development rather than *external* problems with competition and the marketplace.

The Cardiff studies in the UK were therefore designed to focus upon the reality of the position, role and function of marketing as a management function *within* professional service firms.

Organization for marketing

In all three of these studies the majority of respondent firms in each profession reported having some form of organization for marketing (Table 2.1). The implementation of organization for marketing, however, ranges from having a single partner, with marketing as one of a number of specific management responsibilities as well as being a fee earner, to full-blown marketing departments with over twenty employees.

Table 2.1 *Departmentation of marketing*

Is there a marketing department or individual responsible for marketing in your firm?

Accountancy		*Law*		*Consulting engineers*	
Yes (%)	*No* (%)	*Yes* (%)	*No* (%)	*Yes* (%)	*No* (%)
81	19	73	27	56	44
(N=53)		(N=74)		(N=114)	

These organizational arrangements for marketing, however sophisticated or simplistic, were overwhelmingly found to be a product of the 1980s with a large majority being formed within the past five years (Table 2.2).

Table 2.2 *Age of marketing department*

How long has the marketing department/individual responsibility existed?

	One year or less (%)	*Two years* (%)	*Three years or more* (%)	
Accountancy firms	16	19	65	(N=45)
Law firms	52	20	28	(N=54)
Consulting engineering firms	24	30	46	(N=63)

In spite of the organizational responsibilities and arrangements for marketing being relatively young in all three professions the actual number of marketing employees ranged considerably (Table 2.3). From one to over 100 in the accountancy study, one to seven employees in the law firm study and one to nine in the study of consulting engineering firms.

Table 2.3 *Number of marketing employees*

	1 (%)	*2* (%)	*3 or more* (%)	
Accountancy	37	12	51	(N=43)
Law	53	26	21	(N=53)
Consulting engineers	40	19	41	(N=58)

The chief marketing executive and marketing responsibilities

The second major area of the Cardiff studies concerned the head of marketing or classical 'Chief Marketing Executive' (CME) within professional firms. The CME may be seen to be the critical figure since some marketing academics have viewed the marketing concept as simply the orientation of the organization and those integrated activities carried out by the marketing organization and the chief marketing executive (Carson, 1968).[5]

It is clear that in the majority of firms studied the 'chief marketing executive' does have a distinct organizational identity, at least in terms of job title. In most cases the job title of the CME does include the word 'marketing'. The job title of the CME in most firms relates to either marketing partner or marketing director/manager. A number of firms in all professions, but particularly in the accounting profession, choose to relate the CME position to 'practice development' rather than marketing. A number of firms also use 'PR' or 'Public Relations' in the title of the CME's position.

In a number of firms in all professions the organizational responsibility for marketing rests with a committee of partners. In very few firms does such a committee include the word marketing in its title. Some such committees are concerned with 'practice development' but in most cases the committee in question is either the 'executive' or the 'management' committee.

There seems to be something of a dichotomy in the way that professional service firms approach the question of the location of responsibility for marketing within the firm. In firms in which responsibility rests with an individual, whether a partner or a marketing professional, the CME position is specifically related to the functional marketing area in most cases. If, however, the firm locates responsibility for marketing in a committee of partners then this responsibility does not seem to warrant separate functional consideration but is considered in general management committees.

The location of responsibility for the marketing function within the firm and the identification of the position of the chief marketing executive indicates some acknowledgement of marketing as a legitimate issue in professional services management. In terms of the power position of the CME, however, it appears that while the very creation of a CME is an organizational response to the marketing issue by the firm, marketing does not appear to have the internal 'clout' of other management functions within professional service firms.

While an analysis (Table 2.4) of the reporting level of CMEs within professional service firms reveals that the head of marketing within most firms reports only to the highest level of partnership management this does not necessarily convey the relative internal importance of the marketing function.

In most professional service firms, at least in terms of functional management positions, marketing is usually seen to be less important

17

Table 2.4 *CME reporting level*

The CME reports to:

	Accountancy (%)	Law (%)	Engineers (%)
Managing partner	95	23	28
Executive committee	43	58	65
Marketing partner	10	10	7
Development committee	2	9	0

to the management and future of the firm than finance. In many firms marketing is also seen to be less important as a functional area than the personnel function.

The research studies also analysed the role of marketing within professional service firms. This was done specifically in terms of the marketing responsibilities of the chief marketing executive (Table 2.5).

Table 2.5 *CME marketing responsibilities*

	Average responsibility score (5 = full and sole responsibility 1 = no responsibility)		
	Accountancy	Law	Engineering
Advertising	4.2	3.9	3.0
Public relations	4.0	4.1	2.8
Promotion	4.1	4.0	2.9
Marketing planning	3.9	3.7	2.9
New service launch	3.2	3.0	2.2
New service development	3.2	2.7	1.8
Marketing training	3.3	2.8	2.5
Marketing staffing	3.1	2.3	3.0
Marketing research	3.5	1.7	2.8
Corporate planning	2.9	2.7	1.9
Diversification studies	2.7	2.0	2.2
Fee structure	2.3	2.0	1.4
Fee income forecasting	2.2	1.9	1.6

In a number of cases in each of the studies firms felt that particular marketing activities were not applicable in their particular organization. In some cases this was easily explained, e.g. in a firm with only one marketing employee – the marketing director/manager – then marketing staff selection is not a particularly relevant marketing management activity. However, a number of firms in each study felt that marketing training was irrelevant as a function of marketing management and a large number of law firms felt that marketing research was an 'inappropriate' marketing activity in the legal services context.

Marketing textbooks and most professional marketers talk about marketing management activities in terms of the 'marketing mix'. The marketing mix or '4 Ps' as it has become widely known is simply a framework for delineating those management areas that are generally seen to fall within the domain of marketing decision makers. These four areas of the marketing mix are:

- Product
- Price
- Communications *PROMOTION*   ,
- Distribution *PLACE*.

In terms of the activities listed in the studies and the indication of the degree of CME responsibility for each marketing activity, it is easy to see that the CME in the large majority of professional service firms has significant control over only the communications element of the classical marketing mix. Thus decisions relating to the service offerings, fee schedules, office location and service distribution are largely outside the 'domain' of marketing in most professional service firms.

The role of marketing in the strategic direction of firms also appears to be small in comparison to the prescriptive advice of marketing textbooks and the position of most fmcg organizations. While the responsibility scores for marketing planning appear to indicate a strategic role for marketing, subsequent interviews have revealed that this is mainly due to a misunderstanding within the firms studied about what marketing planning entails – most firms relate the activity of marketing planning simply to planning promotional and advertising campaigns. In terms of the other strategic activities – corporate planning and diversification studies – marketing typically had less than equal responsibility with other functions.

The responses to the marketing issue by professional service firms have obviously been many and varied. The studies carried out thus far do, however, show quite clearly that none of the responses match the prescriptions of the 'classical' marketing texts. In organizational terms, the response to the marketing issue seems to be following a relatively similar pattern in a number of professions. We can view the organizational responses to date as a stereotypical model.

Stage 1 – Problem recognition

The managing partner and executive/management committee become aware that increasing competitive pressure and relaxation of professional regulations means that marketing is now a serious issue.

At this stage the senior management's view of the whole issue of marketing and the challenge of the firm's response is characterized by a lack of information and uncertainty.

Stage 2 – Problem allocation

Unable to make any substantial progress with the issue the managing partner and management committee assign the responsibility for marketing to an individual partner who is tasked with collecting information, analysing the issue and formulating the firm's response to marketing. The partner will invariably remain a fee earner and is often one of the newer and more junior members of the partnership.

Stage 3 – Appoint PR consultants

While grappling with the marketing problem and trying to remain an effective fee earner the partner discovers a lack of information about professional services marketing. The partner is visited by a public relations agency who have heard that the firm is looking for information about marketing. The PR consultant impresses the partner with marketing jargon, an apparent understanding of the partner's dilemma and stories of past success (although not usually with PSFs). The agency is duly appointed.

Stage 4 – Appoint internal marketer

After a period of time the marketing budget rises to such a level that the marketing partner begins to argue for a full-time marketing manager. This will ensure that the marketing budget is spent more effectively and free more time for the marketing partner to get on with the 'real' business of generating fees. A marketing manager is appointed – often the PR consultant who handled the firm's account or someone with a similar background.

Stage 5 – Form marketing department

The marketing manager expands the marketing budget and requires an assistant. A marketing assistant, usually either a relatively in-experienced graduate or an ex-secretary to the marketing partner/manager is appointed. The firm now has a partner responsible for marketing, a marketing manager, a marketing assistant and usually a secretary – a *de facto* marketing department.

Some may view this stereotypical model as the cynical observation of an idealistic academic. The majority of the readers of this book will, however, probably recognize at least the general direction of the development of marketing within their firms and in many cases the specific stages of evolution.

There is a sense in which the stereotypical response of most professional service firms to the marketing issue is one of abdication of responsibility. The challenge of marketing to many professional service firms represents a large 'black box' filled with myths and half-truths, ambiguity in terms of the role of professionals and marketing, a dearth of information from both within and outside the profession, budget implications for the partnership and above all a surrounding background of uncertainty. Unable to face the uncertainty around the marketing 'black box' the responsibility is shifted from senior management of firm to individual partner, from marketing partner first to outside consultant and then to internal marketer who will further delegate many marketing tasks to subordinates and outside consultants.

In my experience once responsibility has been 'boxed' and shifted elsewhere (further down the organization in most cases) then it is incredibly difficult to move responsibility back up the organization as it is now 'somebody else's (usually a named individual's) problem'. Many of the problems faced by professional marketers when they join professional service firms relate to their attempts to make people further up the organization recognize their role in marketing and take responsibility for making it happen. These issues will be tackled in depth later, in the final part of the book.

The reality of the function of marketing in the large majority of professional service firms seems to revolve around marketing communications of various kinds: brochures, public relations, press releases, advertisements, etc., and the role of marketing in its current form is to attract new clients. While communications is obviously one of the four elements of the marketing mix it is *only* one element and in the professional service context it is not the most important element of the mix.

The role of marketing in the management and development of professional service firms is severely limited in most cases. While in most professions it can be argued that marketing as a legitimate issue is still in its infancy, the future of marketing within the professions will by no means sort itself out simply over time. There is a distinct danger, which I have witnessed on a number of occasions, that marketing in its current form in many firms will be deemed to have 'failed'. Marketing individuals and departments whose function is built around external marketing communications will require relatively large budgets. As with all marketing expenditure in service businesses the marketers within the firm will be unable to point to changes in bottom line firm performance and directly attribute them to marketing communications. Marketing is then in the organizational position of being seen by many partnerships as a function that spends a good deal of their hard-earned fee income while being unable to tangibly demonstrate a return for the firm on their investment. Therefore the firm may decide that it has 'tried marketing' and found it not to be the panacea promised by the public relations consultants and consequently decide either to abandon marketing or simply curtail its budget.

The reality is, of course, that such firms have not 'tried marketing' at all. They have tried 'marketing communications' and discovered that they can be expensive and that it is very difficult to measure the results tangibly.

The role and function of marketing obviously has the potential to achieve far more in every professional service firm. I have yet to discover a professional service firm in which marketing has taken the firm as far as its potential allows. The role for marketing that has the greatest benefit for the firm as a whole is that of developing a client orientation.

Market orientation and client orientation in the context of professional service firms relate to one and the same thing – defining clients' needs and utilizing the firm's resources as effectively as possible to fill these client needs. Developing a client or market orientation is in many ways the operationalization of marketing and the marketing concept. In this role marketing spends more of its time upon internal activities such as marketing training, communicating research and analyses and driving the corporate planning process than upon writing press releases and designing brochures. This role for marketing has yet to be appreciated and recognized by the vast majority of professional service firms.

The logic of this approach to the role and potential of marketing is simple. The success of any business enterprise in the long term depends upon its ability to create satisfied customers. Few would argue with this logic. The current organization and cultural orientation of most professional service firms are not compatible with achieving this goal. Most firms are organized around functional and service areas that focus upon efficiency in producing a service rather than around the best way to solve a client's problem from the client's point of view. The organizational culture in firms is also usually incompatible with a client orientation, with professionals bounded by an 'us' and 'them' mentality, often accompanied by a feeling of superiority.

In its client orientation role marketing works internally as a change agent, creating and using opportunities to change the professional culture and firm structure in ways which will give clients the perception that the firm is working to solve client problems in the best possible way. I have likened the first stages of this role to marketing being the 'client's voice' within the firm, fighting to make the client's needs and wishes heard and satisfied by those within the firm with the necessary skills, expertise and resource.

While this view challenges the common perception of marketing held by most professionals, few will argue with the logic of the argument and the potential of marketing in this role of client orientation change agent is more obviously seen as a guide to the scope of marketing activities that should be undertaken within the firm and the benefits to the firm of developing such a framework for marketing.

References

1 Stafford, D.C. (1988), 'Advertising in the professions: a review of the literature' *International Journal of Advertising*, vol. 7, pp. 189–220.
2 Shimp, T. A. and Dyer, R. F. (1978), 'How the legal profession views advertising', *Journal of Marketing*, vol. 42, July, pp. 74–81; Smith, R. E. and Meyer, T. S. (1980), 'Attorney advertising: a consumer perspective', *Journal of Marketing*, vol. 44, April; Upah, G. D. and Uhr, E. B. (1981), 'Advertising by public accountants: a review and evaluation of copy strategy' in *Marketing of Services* (eds Donnell, J. H. and George, W. R.), Chicago: AMA; Traynor, K. (1983), 'Accountant advertising: perceptions, attitudes and behaviours', *Journal of Advertising Research*, vol. 23, no. 6, pp.35–40; Carver, M. R. and King, T. E. (1984), 'CPA advertising: how successful has it been', *Financial Executive*, September, pp. 34–42.
3 Watkins, T. and Wright, M. (1985), 'Firm and industry effects of advertising accountancy services', *The Service Industries Journal* vol. 6, no. 3, November, pp. 307–321; Hind, D. W. E. (1986), 'Communication strategies and the accountancy profession: An empirical study', *The Service Industries Journal*, vol. 6, no. 3, November, pp. 309–321; Diamantopoulos, A., O'Donohoe, S. and Lane, J. (1987), 'A path model of the advertising management process among accountants', University of Edinburgh Working Paper Series 88/18.
4 George W. R. and Soloman, P. J. (1980), 'Marketing strategies for improving practice development', *Journal of Accountancy*, February, pp. 79–84; Hughes, M. A. and Kasulis, J. J. (1985), 'The production cue hypothesis and the marketing of legal services', *in Proceedings of American Institute for Decision Services*, pp. 112–116; Lynn, S. A. (1987), 'Identifying buying influences for a professional service: implications for marketing efforts' *Industrial Marketing Management*, vol. 16, no. 2, May.
5 Carson, D. (1968), 'Marketing organisation in British manufacturing firms', *Journal of Marketing*, vol. 32, April, pp. 34–39.

Part Two
Market Analysis and Information

Many writers and analysts of marketing have pointed to marketing as a management function occupying a boundary-spanning role in the organization. It is possible to view marketing acting in functional terms as a buffer between the firm and its environment.

The firm	Marketing	The environment
– Professional service providers	– Marketing strategies	– Existing clients
– Resources	– Marketing programmes	– Potential clients
– Administration		– Competitors
– Expertise	– Marketing information	– Regulation
– Support staff		– Business conditions, etc.

In the simple terms of definitions of marketing and the marketing concept, the marketing function in this boundary-spanning position plays a vital role in enabling the firm to match its internal resources and strengths with the needs of clients in the marketplace in a way that is consistent with the other factors in the business environment.

As part of this boundary-spanning role and in pursuance of the best possible match between the firm and its environment, marketing obviously has an important information-processing role. As the firm's 'window' on its marketplace the marketing function has to collect information from the environment, analyse the information and share it with decision makers in the firm. Indeed if we look back to the definition of marketing presented in Chapter 1, then we can see that the essence of both the definition and philosophy of marketing is meeting client needs. In this sense it is possible to see market analysis and information as the first step in the firm's marketing process since it is the only mechanism for accurately identifying, defining and analysing exactly what it is that existing and potential clients do want, other than intuition and guesswork which are so often and disastrously relied upon in professional service firms.

Chapter 3 introduces professionals to the whole area of market analysis focusing particularly upon the issues of how clients purchase professional services and the factors that influence professional service firm selection for both organizational and consumer clients. This foundation is built upon in the following chapter concerning marketing information and research which concentrates upon the particular problems that professionals seem to face in obtaining and using relevant marketing information, including planning formal marketing research projects.

3 Market analysis

A definition of what exactly constitutes a market very much depends upon the perspective of the discipline involved. Finance people talk about markets as buyers and sellers of stocks, shares, debts, money, currency, etc., while economists describe markets in terms of an aggregate demand of potential buyers for a particular good or service. In marketing in general, and in this book in particular, a more pragmatic approach is taken. A market, in the context of professional services, is a collection of organizations and people with needs that can be filled by a particular type of professional service, that are able to purchase a professional service to satisfy their need.

This definition of a market while appearing relatively straightforward is almost as important for what it does not say as for what it does.

1 It does not say that people and organizations in a market necessarily recognize their own need. Every professional service provider when given the opportunity to meet and talk with an individual or organizational client is able to identify client needs that the client has yet to realize. Discovering potential needs that are not made explicit, or sometimes not even recognized by clients themselves, is obviously a difficult task but it is part of the market analysis function of marketing.

2 The definition does not say that even when an individual or organization recognizes a need that there is a recognition that this need can be satisfied by a type of professional service firm. This indicates a role not only in the analysis of markets in order to plan information/education communications to such potential clients by individual firms but also a responsibility of professional bodies and associations to undertake such analysis and communications programmes for the benefit of the whole of the profession.

3 While the market definition explicitly identifies *ability* to pay for professional service solutions, it does not identify a *willingness* to pay professional service fees in order to benefit from satisfaction of their needs. The identification and analysis of client buying behaviour in order to plan marketing strategies and programmes is again an information-processing function of the role of marketing in the professional service context.

From the marketing point of view total markets such as the world market for architectural services or the UK market for legal services are almost meaningless. The reasons for this and marketing's response in terms of segmentation are, for reasons which will become apparent, discussed in Chapter 7. However, many firms do like to know their position in the 'big picture' of the total marketplace with some notion that this will give stimulus to strategic thinking on the part of partners to improve the position of their firm in the total market. While this may produce meaningful figures for a very small number of the world's largest accountancy firms, thinking about total global markets in relation to specific firms is not a useful exercise – I would even argue that it is not a useful strategic exercise for those few accountancy firms who can produce meaningful figures.

Total aggregate markets contain so many market variables and submarkets that we are simply unable to alter or influence that they can distort our view of where we are now and where it is possible for us to go. I was asked to visit a west country law firm after the senior partner had read an article that I had published, to discuss the potential benefits of strategic marketing planning for the firm. I was ushered into a boardroom to face the four partners who made up the executive committee of the firm. The atmosphere was distinctly adversarial and unfriendly as I began talking about marketing and its role in the development of professional firms. Eventually one of the partners spoke up and asked me how it was possibly relevant to talk about marketing strategies for this firm when the firm had only a .001 per cent share of the market in which it operates. I was momentarily stunned at this interjection before I realized the significance of the partner's comment and its relationship with the hostile air around the meeting.

After some discussion I was able to change the atmosphere of the meeting and the executive committee's views on the relevance of strategic marketing planning simply by breaking down the partners' market share perceptions. Having reduced the aggregate market figures, first by looking at the actual geographic market for its services and then by the types of service it offered, we were able to negotiate realistic and meaningful figures for the firm's penetration of its 'competed' market, i.e. the potential marketplace for its existing professional service offerings through its current distribution of offices (Figure 3.1). The firm actually turned out to have a 12 per cent share of this competed market which enabled the partners to see the relevance of market share figures as a goal setting and control mechanism, and to see that marketing could potentially affect their position in this 'competed' market in a way that would be meaningless in terms of the aggregate market.

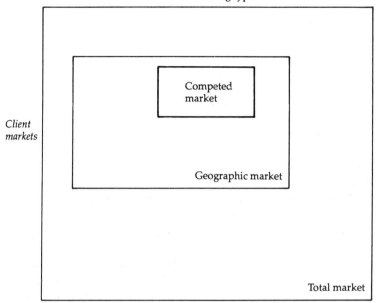

Service offering types

Client
markets

Competed
market

Geographic market

Total market

Figure 3.1 *Total market vs competed market*

Without defining some market parameters and sizing markets
realistically, even if only in terms of orders of magnitude, most
professionals within PSFs will continue to see marketing as something
of a 'black box' that swallows up partnership funds with no tangible
way of necessarily influencing the firm's position in its marketplace.
While the uncertainty surrounding the size and parameters of the
actual market in which the firm operates remains it will be very difficult
to convince partners that marketing can reasonably set explicit targets
against which the partnership can measure the performance and
effectiveness of their marketing efforts. This is not to say that
measuring marketing performance is as simple as setting market share
goals against which to control. Marketing has a number of functions in
using resources to create intangible assets which are difficult to define,
let alone measure, such as firm image, name awareness, etc. These
things are *intangible* assets and they do play a part in the firm's business
development. They are, however, by their very nature, difficult to
measure quantitatively. This should not lead us into the trap of
dismissing the importance of the creation, sustenance and development of these intangibles' assets. Just because they are difficult to
measure does not mean that they are not important. This cannot be
dismissed as idealistic academic nonsense. Some of the most analytical

and financially astute minds in the country are located in the City and the City consistently, through its share valuations, places a high cash value upon just such intangible assets as brand names.

Having established the 'competed' market in which a firm operates in order to remove some of the uncertainty that surrounds the present and potential future position of a firm vis-à-vis its marketplace we can return to what is perhaps the most fundamental part of market analysis in the way that it relates to adopting the marketing concept – analysing client behaviour.

Analysing client behaviour

Market analysis necessarily focuses much attention upon the key area of the buying behaviour of existing and potential clients. It can be seen that more particularly, market analysis involves the study of how and why potential clients become the clients of particular professional service firms or seek the help/advice of a type of professional service firm. Many professional service firms have client bases that include both individuals and corporate clients. This will involve professional service firms in analysing the buying behaviour of both individual consumers and organizations. With clients of both types there are a number of questions to be addressed by professional service firms if they are to successfully negotiate this first stage of developing a marketing orientation.

- What exactly does the client need?
- What type of buying decision is this?
- What factors influence the buying decision?

Client needs

In terms of client needs there is a large degree of congruence between some of the general characteristics surrounding client needs in both individual and organizational buying behaviour.

The nature of the work of most professionals and the generic context of the professional services marketplace means that in all cases client needs are surrounded by a degree of uncertainty as far as the client is concerned.[1] Many professional marketers will be familiar with the comment from the Revlon company in the USA, 'In the factory we make cosmetics – in the store we sell hope'. This sort of analogy also applies to the professional services context because of the nature of client uncertainty. In 'product' terms most professional service firms produce technical solutions to complex problems, but from the client's point of view the benefit he/she derives from purchasing a professional service is primarily a reduction of the uncertainty surrounding the problem. Thus the product as far as the client is concerned is 'confidence', i.e. that he or she can confidently leave the problem resolution to the staff of the professional service firm. Viewing 'confidence' as the primary benefit sought by clients can have a dramatic effect in the way that a firm interfaces with the client since it allows the firm to see what is really important to the client. This approach will be discussed in more detail in Chapter 12.

Users and potential users of professional services are by definition exhibiting a degree of uncertainty. The *raison d'être* of professional services is providing expertise in the form of qualified and experienced professionals to formulate solutions to problems that are usually beyond the technical capability of the user, e.g. an individual will approach a law firm to provide a conveyancing service when he or she is selling and/or buying a property largely because that individual does not possess the knowledge, technical expertise and experience to perform the conveyancing service for themselves. Being unable to perform the service for themselves leads clients to be uncertain about the process of conveyancing and the timing, cost and even the nature of the outcome. In most cases clients will even require the assistance of professionals in order to ascertain the problem itself.

Allied to the client's problem in being usually unable to perform the professional service required without the help of a professional service firm, is the intangible nature of the service offering. Since clients are usually less technically competent in the particular area in which they are seeking professional service help than the professional staff of the PSFs, the client has a problem in deciding upon which particular PSF is the most likely to produce the best solution for his problem. Thus the intangibility of professional service offerings leads to even greater uncertainty on the part of the client. Not only is the client likely to be uncertain about the problem itself but also about how to choose an effective professional service provider to solve the problem. This surrounding uncertainty is further increased by the importance of the problem resolution to either the individual or the organizational client and the relative size of the fee likely to be demanded by the professional service firm.

Uncertainty can be seen to be a characteristic of both organizational and individual clients of professional service firms. In most cases it can be seen that clients are actually buying the professional's ability to reduce this uncertainty rather than any technical expertise or capability. If this is the case then marketing has a leading role to play in moving the firm away from a functional/technical approach to its service offering towards an approach based upon the actual benefit derived by the client who utilizes the service. Marketing also has a direct external role in identifying sources of client uncertainty and using the firm's communications mix to reduce client uncertainty and boost confidence wherever possible.

While organizational and individual clients of PSFs do share some common characteristics in their approach to buying professional services, some important differences necessitate looking at the buying behaviour and decision processes of each in turn.

It is obviously impossible to model accurately the behaviour and decision making process of all types of buyers of professional services. A number of frameworks have been developed, however, that do give a potentially useful insight into the buying behaviour of both corporate and individual clients.

Organizational buyer behaviour

Since organizational clients can be as diverse as anything from a one-man ice-cream vendor through large multinational corporations and charitable institutions, to governments, it may seem nonsensical to talk about 'organizational clients' as if it were some sort of homo-geneous group of users of professional services. While this is certainly true, one can establish frameworks that are valuable in the analysis of the market for a professional service firm and that can produce insights upon which to base effective marketing programmes and marketing strategies.

One such framework concerns the actual buying decision that is faced by the client. The actual buying decisions faced by clients will obviously vary enormously in size, risk, complexity, time-scale, etc., and these variables within a typology of decision making must be examined by professional service firms, for they will have major implications for the role that the PSF is to play, and suggest activities and tasks that are appropriate. Many schemes classifying buying decisions have been attempted in the past but perhaps the most robust and widely used is that suggested by Robinson et al.[2] These researchers formulated a typology of decision situations faced by organizational buyers which identified three distinct buying situations.

New task purchases

This type of buying decision is faced by organizational buyers when the organization needs to use a professional service that is unfamiliar to the organization, i.e. they have a limited experience in using this type of professional service. This can often mean that the organization is also unfamiliar with providers of the new professional service, e.g. a company that has occupied a leased factory site to date, that decides that it wishes to have a new facility built will be unfamiliar with how to set about approaching architects, surveyors, etc., and will probably have very little experience of these types of professional service providers.

New task buying decisions are usually characterized by a very high degree of buyer uncertainty as they are usually more complex and unfamiliar than other types of buying situation. Buyers facing new task decisions will require as much information as possible from professional service providers in order to reduce this uncertainty. Buying decisions of this kind will usually involve consideration of a larger number of types of professional service that may be able to offer a potential solution to their new task problem, e.g. in the above example the company will consider whether to approach an architect, a surveyor or a building contractor as a source of a solution to their need of a new facility. Such buyers will also be more likely to contact and consider a larger number of individual firms within a professional service type since they usually have no (or only limited) experience, knowledge and relations with individual PSFs of this kind. Thus in new task purchase decisions organizational buyers will face the greatest uncertainty and will therefore require the most information and help from professionals in making the buying decision. It is also the type of buying decision in which the greatest number of firms will be contacted and compared as potential sources of professional service solutions.

Modified rebuy

In the 'modified rebuy' purchase decision the organizational buyer is faced with the situation of purchasing a professional service for the resolution of a problem with which the organization is at least partially familiar. An example of this type of purchase situation may be the appointment of an accountancy firm for audit as in the past but also to ask the accountants to undertake some tax consultancy work as well. A modified rebuy situation can be seen as an only partly new buying decision. The organizational buyer is likely to have had some experience in purchasing the type of professional service needed to solve their problems and/or some experience of professional service firms providing that type of service. In the above example the organization has certainly appointed auditors before and may even have had tax consultancy services before although this service may not have been provided by the same firm of accountants or may even have been provided by a law firm.

The degree of uncertainty experienced by the organizational buyer in this situation is obviously less than in the new task situation since the buyer has at least some degree of familiarity with either the professional and/or the firms providing the professional service. This lesser degree of uncertainty means that buyers typically require less information in their purchase decisions and will typically consider fewer alternative suppliers of professional services.

Straight rebuy

This type of purchase decision situation can be characterized as a 'repeat purchase' scenario. In the straight rebuy situation the organizational buyer is seeking the provision of a professional service that is very similar to that which it has purchased previously, often on a regular basis, e.g. a company may use a single law firm in its debt recovery efforts. This can become relatively routinized and even if the company gives some of this work to other law firms at times it is still a straight rebuy decision since the company knows the professional service it requires to solve its debt recovery needs and has purchased such services before. Accountancy firms will recognize the appointment and reappointment of auditors as another example of a straight rebuy decision.

These purchase decisions are the easiest to make for organizational buyers since they are characterized by the least uncertainty as the buyer has experienced the purchase decision before and experienced using both the professional service, and in the case of reappointment, the specific service provider as well. Organizations facing such buying decisions are much more likely to use firms that they have used before to provide such services than those facing either modified rebuy or new task purchase decisions.

Each of the three types of buying decision has different implications for the marketing effort of professional service firms. If the organizations identified by the firm as within their target market are facing straight rebuy decisions and are existing clients the marketing approach of the firm is obviously to reinforce their past buying behaviour and purchase decision with close contact in order to encourage a straight reappointment and the minimization of consideration of alternative professional service providers. If the organization facing the straight rebuy decision is not an existing client then the marketing approach is obviously to encourage the consideration of alternatives to existing professional advisors with the provision of competitive positioning information and communication and different perspectives upon the solution of their professional service needs. Most firms will find that 'loyalty' is still a word used by organizations about their existing professional advisors. By this term most organizational buyers in fact mean that the complexity and uncertainty surrounding the purchase of any professional service is such that they wish to go through the process as infrequently as possible and that this leads them to retain professional advisors for long periods of time. Fortunately, such an approach to buying professional services is changing as organizational buyers become increasingly sophisticated in their decision making and in the selection of professional service providers.

Organizations facing modified rebuy and new task purchase situations are of more immediate and obvious interest to professional service firms since both types of purchase decision encourage a wider evaluation and consideration of alternative professional service firms. It is with these types of organizational buying decisions that the PSF's marketing communications are of most importance since the higher degree of buyer uncertainty will lead to a wider and more rigorous information search. With organizations that are existing clients PSFs obviously need to demonstrate competence and encourage client confidence through helping the client to further define his need in professional service terms as quickly and as comprehensively as possible. The quicker the organization's uncertainty can be resolved by the PSF then the less likely clients are to consider alternative professional service approaches and alternative service providers. If the organizations are not existing clients then the PSF obviously needs a quick, direct marketing approach that will allow the firm to present its own definition and understanding of the organization's professional service need in order to encourage evaluation of the firm as a potential service provider alongside the organization's existing professional advisors.

Organizational decision making

The way in which the purchase decision is arrived at within organizations is also of obvious interest to professional service marketers. No professional service firm can seriously expect to influence the organizational purchase decision unless they understand not only the type of buying decision faced but also the process by which the purchase decision is made. A number of frameworks for analysing purchase decision making processes in organizations are available. The framework proposed here (Figure 3.2) has been adapted for the

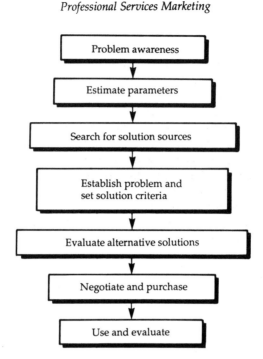

Figure 3.2 *Purchase decision framework*

professional service context from an original model by Wind and Thomas.[3]

Problem awareness

The organizational buying decision process obviously starts with an awareness at some level that the organization is facing a situation or problem for which they may need the help of professional service providers. Although in most cases this awareness develops due to the effects of external conditions and the interaction within the organization, it is possible to stimulate this awareness. If a professional service firm is able to establish the sources of the problem awareness stage in an organization then it may be able to stimulate or influence future problem awareness through its communication efforts that will be picked up in the organization's environmental scanning activities. Many organizations are even 'grateful' to PSFs who can identify the potential impacts of environmental changes that will affect the organization such as regulatory changes, etc. and propose pro-active professional service solutions.

Estimate parameters

Once an organization has internally developed an awareness of a problem that may need a professional service solution it moves into a phase in the decision making process that is characterized by great uncertainty. Simply becoming aware of an internal problem is easy. Defining the problem is often very difficult for organizations. Problems that require professional service solutions are, almost by definition, beyond the capabilities of an organization to define specifically due to lack of technical professional expertise and/or the time and resources to fully analyse the problem. Organizations will typically define their problem only in terms of rough parameters at this stage since they usually lack the competence, confidence and time to do anything else. It is obviously vital at this stage in the decision making process for marketers to present their professional service firm as a source of competence with the ability to help the organization define its problems and to project the PSF as bringing certainty into this uncertain situation within the organization.

Search for sources of solution

Having defined the problem in general terms the organization will then search for potential sources of professional service solutions. Depending upon the organization's familiarity with the problem situation it will typically evaluate which type of professional help is most likely to be useful and which particular firms' service offerings are likely to be suitable. At this stage it is important that the professional bodies themselves disseminate information and communicate widely to allow organizations to decide upon the type of professional service they are most likely to require. At the individual PSF level it is at this stage that the firm's image and perceived competitive position is likely to be of the greatest importance in new task and modified rebuy situations. The organization, having decided upon the type of professional service help it is likely to need, will try to identify a number of firms within a profession that they perceive to have the necessary skills, experience, etc. to solve their problem. Organizations will typically move through this stage as quickly as possible and will not in most cases undertake a systematic search and information gathering exercise to identify objectively the likeliest PSFs for this particular problem. Thus image, perceived positioning and name awareness are very important at this stage.

Problem definition and solution criteria

Having identified a number of firms that are believed to be capable and suitable potential suppliers of a professional service, the organization will then meet, or at least contact, representatives from each firm. The roughly defined problem is presented and discussed with each firm and in many areas a more detailed written evaluation of the organization's problem and the PSF's proposed solution is requested. At this stage of the buying process the organization effectively uses the knowledge and skills of the representatives of each of the PSFs to help them define the nature of their own problem and thus their need for professional service help more precisely. It is vital to understand the organization's need for help in their problem definition activities at this stage. As well as defining its professional service need at this point the organization is also likely to utilize the viewpoints provided by all the PSFs contacted to put together a set of criteria to be addressed by the chosen professional service provider in its solution.

Evaluate alternative solutions

Having contacted a number of potential professional service providers and defined more clearly their problem and professional service need, the organization is now in a position to evaluate the professional service solutions proposed by a number of firms. Most organizations by this stage are a good deal more certain about the nature of their problem and their likely need for professional service. The specific proposals received from the professional service firms are likely to differ, reflecting the viewpoint, background and specific technical skills of the PSF contact. In general, however, the organization will put together a composite idea of their 'core' professional service needs from the various proposals of the potential service providers and this 'core' service need will be a part of the proposals that are seriously considered. Many factors will influence the selection of the specific firm that is chosen as the service provider by the organization but one of the most important in many cases is the knowledge, skill, understanding and insight shown by the PSF in helping the organization to define its problem and thus its professional service need. A professional service firm that can display skill in defining the organization's problem is showing that it can reduce uncertainty for the potential client. This will engender confidence in the PSF which is the key to gaining the client.

Negotiate and purchase

Having chosen the professional service provider the client will now negotiate more specifically the service that it requires and the way in which the service is to be performed. It is at this stage that the specific proposal presented for evaluation alongside those from other PSFs is renegotiated, changed and broken down into a more detailed client service plan. While the fee expected by the PSF will normally have been a part of the proposal evaluated in the previous stage it is often renegotiated here alongside time-scale and the specific staff that will provide the service. Once the details of the client service plan have been agreed the client will instruct the professional service firm to begin acting on its behalf. It is in this phase that the PSF should take every opportunity to redefine what exactly it is that the client needs and customize the original proposal to match the client needs as closely as possible. The face-to-face negotiation and purchase is an excellent opportunity for 'customization' of the professional service offering.

Use and evaluate

In this final phase of the purchase decision cycle the client uses the professional service firm to satisfy its professional service need – whether this is for an individual project or in an ongoing advisory capacity. While using the services of the PSF the client will continuously be evaluating the firm. This evaluation process will usually entail the use of evaluation criteria that are non-technical and often unrelated to the specific need and service being provided. The staff and management of the client firm will be continuously making implicit and explicit judgements about the personalities of the service providers, the way they interact with the staff of the client, the quality of their communications, etc. These qualitative, non-technical, unsystematic evaluations are critical in building a picture of how the client will perceive the experience of using the PSF and hence will be important in decisions relating to retaining the PSF and appointing and considering the PSF for future assignments.

This framework of organizational decision making suggests a number of stages in which different marketing activities and efforts are appropriate for professional service firms. It also highlights the fact that in choosing a professional service firm organizations will usually arrive at a choice in an unsystematic, irrational and even emotional way. Any professional service firm that believes that potential clients choose between firms in a systematic, rational and economic manner are guilty of the worst kind of marketing ignorance – being out of tune with the reality of the client and his world.

What factors influence the purchase decision?

Having discussed the types of purchase situations faced by organizations and established a framework of the purchase decision making process, it is obviously vital for professional service firms to understand the factors that can and do influence organizational purchase decisions.

In the organizational context the purchase decision is often made by a group of people rather than a single person. It is obviously necessary for the PSF to identify this decision making unit, its members and the role that they play in the decision making process. In some cases a specific decision making unit (DMU) will exist and this identification will be relatively straightforward, e.g. an audit committee or property development committee. In other organizations the DMU may be more informal in nature but in organizations of any size it is rare that the purchase decision will be taken entirely by an individual. Researchers in the USA have identified five roles that are typically found in the purchase decision making unit (Webster and Wind):[4]

Users those who will actually interact with the professional service providers and will receive and use the professional service help.
Buyers those with formal responsibility for purchasing decisions of this type.
Influencers those who influence the decision making process by supplying information and criteria that can be used in making the purchase decision.
Deciders those with authority to choose amongst potential service providers.
Gatekeepers those who can control the flow of information into the decision making unit and thus influence both the purchase decision process and its outcome.

While these roles have been identified as discrete roles, in many organizations more than one individual may perform a single role and in many cases a single individual may perform a number of roles. The role of the professional service marketer is obviously to identify those performing the above role functions within potential client organizations and plan the marketing effort to target each individual in order to exert the maximum influence upon the decider/buyer that will take the critical end decision of which PSF to use.

This particular model provided some real insight and leverage in terms of developing a marketing strategy during a marketing audit undertaken for a large and established firm of civil engineers. This firm had been receiving an increasing number of small verification jobs from the in-house structural design unit of a very large pharmaceuticals manufacturer that had been a client of the civil engineering firm since its main UK plant had been built some fifteen years ago.

The drawings that had been received for verification by the firm made it obvious that substantial building work was being undertaken yet the firm had received no new civil projects from the manufacturer at all. A simple analysis of the purchase decision making unit in the manufacturer explained this situation and left the firm with a set of concrete marketing activities that eventually resulted in a number of large civil engineering projects.

The implicit assumption that undertaking the verification work for the manufacturer would lead to them being considered for the resulting construction projects proved to be completely unfounded. It was quickly ascertained that the manufacturer was involved in a major reorganization consolidating all European manufacturing operations into the UK site. The key figure in the purchase decision making unit proved to be a senior project engineer (who the firm never even knew existed!) and the manufacturer's structural design unit played no role in the purchase decision at all other than getting their own drawings and plans verified, which was considered to be a completely independent, and important, task within the manufacturer. The purchase decision making unit in the manufacturer that emerged is shown in Figure 3.3.

This analysis led to a recognition that the key figure in the purchase decision process for civil engineering services was the senior project engineer – someone with whom the firm in question had never even spoken. A meeting with the senior project engineer revealed that he was greatly influenced by particular articles in magazines such as *Engineering Today*, *Building Today* and *Project Engineer* that described specific projects undertaken by firms and especially those undertaken in sterile manufacturing environments. The other influencers in the decision were primarily negative in that they only provided an input in terms of 'I don't care who you appoint, as long as it isn't "Joe Bloggs & Co".' It was also revealed that a competing civil engineering firm had recently impressed the senior project engineer by simply providing a free proposal when they learned of an imminent civil project through a friend within the firm.

This relatively simple analysis led to the firm changing its position on preparing detailed written proposal and draft plans before a contract was awarded, a number of articles upon specific projects that

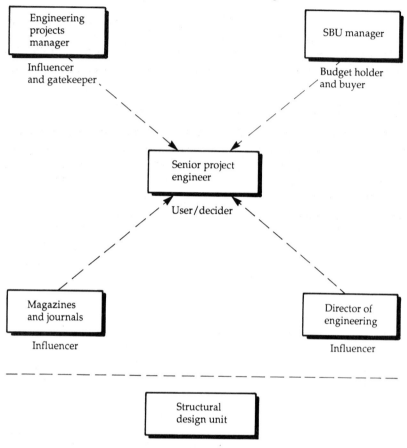

Figure 3.3 *Purchase decision making unit for civil engineering services*

were felt to be interesting in the journals, and a series of lunches, etc. with influencers with the particular manufacturer. Within twelve months the firm received a number of the civil engineering projects from the manufacturer and new projects began to come through from unsolicited enquiries as a direct result of the articles in the relevant journals.

Decision making units in purchase decisions for professional services are, however, likely to be different between professions, industrial sectors and even from company to company within sectors. Recent research in the USA[5] has shown that the number of participants in the purchase decision process for auditor selection can range from 1 to 14. Thus the precise number, location and role played by decision participants is likely to differ between individual clients as well as between professional services.

Research into the factors influencing the selection of professional service firms has been undertaken by marketing academics. Most of this work, however, has been undertaken in the USA. While the specific results of much of the available research may be deemed to be inappropriate to the specific context of the UK, the results are nonetheless interesting and informative for those involved in marketing professional services in the UK.

In the accountancy profession one of the most comprehensive pieces of market analysis publicly available was undertaken by Tyebjee and Bruno in 1982.[6] This study focused upon the importance of factors in the selection of accountancy firms amongst small and medium-sized hi-technology companies (Table 3.1).

Table 3.1 *Criteria involved in selection decision (small/medium hi-tech companies)*

Criterion	Mean importance[1]
Rapport with personnel of CPA firm	2.7
Whether audit and tax partners give personal attention	2.6
Speed with which services are provided	2.6
The amount of the fee	2.4
Whether a smooth transition to a new CPA firm is possible	2.2
The extent to which the firm specializes in the electronics industry	2.1
Opinion of friends and colleagues	2.1
Whether a management letter is provided	1.9
Sales presentations by the CPA firm	1.7
Promotional literature from the CPA firm	1.5
Whether the CPA firm has international offices	1.4
Number of branch offices	1.3

[1]The range of importance scores rises to a maximum of 3 on a three point scale.

A wider study undertaken by George and Solomon in 1980[7] with a larger number of bigger organizations in a number of industrial sectors used different measures and achieved different results as shown in Table 3.2.

Table 3.2 *Criteria involved in selection decision (large industrial organizations)*

Criterion	Rank	Median
Specialization of CPA firm in the industry	1	2.9
Recommendations from other clients of the CPA firm	2	3.6
Aggressiveness of the CPA firm	3	4.3
Current client list of the CPA firm	4	4.6
CPA firm is one of 'Big 8'	5	4.7
Fee estimates given by CPA firm	6	5.1
Belief that CPA firm will give the company an unqualified opinion	7	5.9
Friendships with members of CPA firm	8	6.4
Community activities by members of CPA firm	9	8.2
Club memberships and entertainment by members of the CPA firm	10	9.1

The differences between these two studies demonstrate that there is no single answer to that question which I am asked most often about market analysis by professionals 'Why do clients choose one firm rather than another?' The research into PSF selection that has been undertaken shows that the importance of various criteria in the fifth stage of our organizational purchase decision making process varies not only between professions but also with client size and industrial sector. This points towards the need for marketing research in the market analysis activities of PSFs which will be further developed in the next chapter.

In the legal profession I have myself carried out some research into the factors influencing firm selection by organizational clients.[8] This research was carried out in 1989 amongst companies from a wide variety of industrial sectors and of widely different sizes. The results are summarized in Table 3.3.

Table 3.3 *Importance of factors in choosing a law firm*

Factor	Mean score
Professional and technical skills	1.08
Partner accessibility	1.56
Range of service provided by firm	2.02
Geographic proximity to firm	2.22
Firm's proposal and fee	2.30
Specialization in type of service	2.33
Local reputation	2.58
Industry specialization	2.66
National standing	2.99
Word-of-mouth recommendation	3.14
Third party referral	3.16
International network	3.67
Current client list	4.03

In the engineering profession the only publicly available research that I have found was undertaken in Canada in 1974 by Sarkar and Saleh[9] amongst buyers of consulting engineering services in the municipal sector. The results of this study, which again used different measurements, are displayed in Table 3.4.

These pieces of research demonstrate the diversity of the factors that organizations use to evaluate potential service providers. While this information will be of interest to readers in the UK, and may well help partners in professional service firms to begin thinking substantially about the criteria for evaluation that might be used in their own marketplaces, it highlights the need for each firm to undertake a thorough analysis of its own marketplace.

It must also be remembered that in the majority of situations only a limited number of firms of potential professional service providers will

Table 3.4 *Criteria used in selection of consulting engineers*

Criterion	Importance
Competence factors:	
Competence	High
Experience	Very high
Adequate staff	Medium
Concept of problem	High
Knowledge of local condition	Very high
Technical reputation	High
Fees	Medium
Personality factors:	
Engineer's personality	Very low
Co-operation	Medium
Objectives	Low
Professional standing	Medium
Civic reputation	Low
Integrity (honesty)	High

reach the stage of being evaluated by organizational clients and PSFs cannot escape the simple fact that unless organizations in a particular marketplace are aware of the firm and can identify readily, and without much information-seeking effort, its positioning in terms of size, specialization and quality vis-à-vis other firms, then the firm is unlikely to be considered as a potential service provider. In this context some research has been conducted into the criteria used to evaluate PSFs in the accountancy, legal and banking sectors by those organizations asked to recommend a professional service firm.[10] The results of this study, shown in Table 3.5, again demonstrate a different set of criteria, with different relative importances, used by referral sources who are obviously an important marketing target. In many cases it is the referral source that can move the professional service firm, in the eyes of the organizational client, to the position where it will be evaluated as a potential service provider alongside others.

Table 3.5 *Criteria used by referral sources to evaluate PSFs*

Variable description	Mean score[1]
Qualification of personnel	4.455
Expertise in client's area of need	4.444
Commitment to ethics	4.421
Ability to meet deadlines	4.252
Personal acquaintance	3.953
Accessibility of top management	3.567
Reasonableness of fee structure	3.533
Range of services provided	3.236
Size relative to the client	2.988
Probability of referral reciprocation	2.941
Location of office(s)	2.519

[1](5 = Very important; 1 = Not important)

Consumer buying behaviour

While for many types of professional service firms organizational clients are the most important clients in terms of fee income and high margin business, for a number of professionals (and for smaller firms within each profession) individual consumers may be an important source of revenue. The earlier discussion of client needs applies equally to both corporate and consumer clients; in terms of buying decision types and processes there are, however, different frameworks that can be identified which may be of use to marketers of consumer professional service firms.

Types of consumer purchase decisions

In much the same way as discussed earlier in terms of organizational buyers, individual consumers can be seen as facing different purchase situations in terms of familiarity, complexity and uncertainty surrounding the need and purchase of a professional service. A framework incorporating these variables has been proposed by Howard and Sheth.[11] In this framework it is suggested that most consumers face three possible kinds of purchase situation. Although this framework was not derived from analyses of consumers of professional services it is potentially applicable to the professional service context.

Routinized response behaviour

This is the simplest purchase situation faced by consumers of professional services. In these buying situations the consumer is faced with a familiar professional service need that he/she has satisfied before with a professional service purchase. Given the consumer's experience with this type of buying situation they do not typically expend a large amount of time or effort exploring alternative solutions and professional service providers. Good examples of routinized response behaviour are going to the dentist for a regular check-up, taking a pet to the vet for a booster innoculation, etc. In most purchase situations of this type the consumer has an established relationship with a professional service provider.

Limited problem solving

This type of purchase situation is typified by a consumer who is purchasing a familiar professional service, e.g. medical, dental, accounting, legal, etc., from an unfamiliar professional service firm. This situation is also faced by consumers purchasing unfamiliar services from a familiar professional, e.g. seeking pension planning advice from his or her lawyers. Obviously this type of need situation arises when a consumer moves into a new area, is unsatisfied with past professional service providers or when his or her circumstances change resulting in a new need for an existing professional service. In such situations consumers are typically much more likely to engage in some search process for information about potential service providers or the services offered by existing providers.

Extensive problem solving

This type of buying situation is typically the most complex for consumers and is characterized by the most uncertainty. In this situation the consumer is faced with an unfamiliar professional service need that is unlikely to be filled by providers with whom the consumer has experience, e.g. an individual wishing to have a house built is unlikely to have come across a personal need to choose an architect before. Similarly a consumer with a serious health problem may have no experience in specialist medical advice and services. In such purchase situations the consumer is likely to spend much time and effort exploring potential professional service solutions and alternative professional service suppliers.

Each of these purchase situations is likely to be faced by the individual clients of professional service firms and each suggests different focuses of the firm's marketing effort, and the role of marketing in the development of the firm.

In the routinized response behaviour situation the most obvious role of marketing is to ensure that clients of the firm remain clients of the firm. This will involve current client research, identification of cases of dissatisfaction, the maintenance of expected service quality and the constant reinforcement of the consumer's initial buying decision to purchase service from the firm. In the limited problem-solving situation this role of marketing is extended and will necessitate more of a marketing communications and personal selling effort in order to make current clients aware of the other services provided by the firm that might be useful to the consumer. Marketers will also wish to focus marketing communications efforts upon those moving into the area and referral sources may be important marketing targets in this situation. In the extensive problem-solving scenario marketers will obviously wish to ensure that information about the firm is easy to obtain and that it clearly positions the firm in terms of expertise, personnel, fees, etc. In extensive problem solving the ability of the firm to take part in identifying the consumer's problem and potential professional service solutions will also be a services marketing effort.

The consumer purchase decision process

In any of the purchase decision situations faced by the individual consumer there are a number of stages through which he or she will pass in their decision making process before choosing a supplier of a professional service. The importance of each stage of this process in terms of the degree of effort the consumer is willing to expend will obviously vary enormously, and in different purchase situations consumers may even skip or combine stages in the purchase decision process. The consumer purchase decision process is typically less complex than the organizational decision process that we examined earlier. Most consumer purchase decision frameworks will include the steps shown in Figure 3.4.

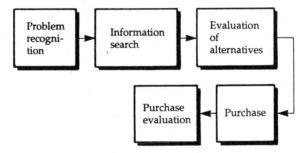

Figure 3.4 *Consumer purchase decision process*

Problem recognition

This is the beginning of the consumer purchase decision model where the individual identifies a problem or a need that he/she would like solved or satisfied. In most cases this problem recognition or identification of a need stage can be reached by either an 'internal cue' such as a feeling of illness or an injury, or an 'external cue' such as a regulatory requirement for VAT returns or conveyancing, etc. Marketers are obviously interested in identifying the types of cues that bring individuals in their own marketplace to the problem recognition stage that results in the identification of a need for a professional service.

Information search

Having identified a need, a consumer will seek information upon various ways in which the need may be satisfied. Information searches may range from simply looking up the number of your family doctor in the routinized response situation to ringing professional bodies and individual firms for information, brochures, etc. with numerous stages of effort and complexity in-between. Marketers will be keen to examine the information-searching activities of consumers in their target market in order to best utilize their marketing communication resources.

Evaluation of alternatives

Having collected and analysed information from the information search stage the consumer will feel able to identify potential professional service providers that may be able to solve their problem or fulfil their professional service need. The actual criteria used in making a choice between a set of potential service providers will differ between different types of need. However, in most cases consumers will evaluate upon criteria that enable them to feel confidence and less uncertainty in the service provider, e.g. years of experience, personal experience of firm, referral from a friend or colleague, etc. Typically, less research has been conducted into the evaluation of professional service providers in the consumer marketplace than in the corporate marketplace. One research study in the United States, however, suggested that male consumers are more likely to use tangible external cues in their evaluation than women.[12] Some of the results of this research are shown in Table 3.6 which depicts the importance of factors in the evaluation of potential providers of legal services.

Table 3.6 *Factors important in the evaluation of potential providers*

Middle income males	Mean	Others	Mean
Years of experience	5.92	Personable qualities	5.69
Speciality	5.74	Speciality	5.48
Personable qualities	5.55	Years of experience	5.49
Recommendation	4.90	Recommendation	5.02
Acquaintance	4.86	Acquaintance	4.96
Convenient hours	4.57	Convenient hours	4.40
Convenient location	4.28	Convenient location	4.37

Purchase

The evaluation of potential service providers along the criteria favoured by the consumer will lead to the identification of a favoured provider. The translation of this favoured provider into the actual supplier of a professional service is achieved through the purchase phase. This may indeed be the first time that the potential client contacts the firm and the translation from favoured candidate to actual supplier may not be an easy or straightforward process. In contacting the firm the potential client may decide that he/she doesn't like the tone/personality of the firm or individual professional simply from a telephone call and may call another firm. Often the availability of the service at a convenient time will cause the client to switch from the originally preferred provider to another firm. Marketers will need to know the obstacles and factors that can prevent a potential client becoming an actual client as the firm will obviously wish to reduce these barriers and perceptions with regard to its own potential clients and even analyse how the firm might best profit from these factors with potential clients of competing firms.

Purchase evaluation

After purchase and during and after using a professional service the consumer will formulate an opinion as to the wisdom of the choice of professional service provider and gain some awareness of the firm and its staff which will reshape their initial perceptions and lead to a feeling of satisfaction or dissatisfaction with the firm and its service provision. Most consumers will have a heavy emotional rather than rational component in their purchase decision making and will thus look for clues and evidence that their purchase decision was the 'correct' one. This demonstrates the need for marketers to reinforce the original beliefs of the client as much as possible. Marketers will also need to determine the actual criteria and relative importance of the factors used by consumers in evaluating the quality of the professional service offering and in reaching a decision concerning their satisfaction with their original purchase decision. An approach to this question is discussed in Chapter 12.

Market analysis is the cornerstone of successful marketing. It is obviously the first stage in the marketing process and the development of a marketing orientation within a professional service firm. Unfortunately, market analysis is not a quick, easy or glamorous task. The market analysis phase of any strategic or marketing planning process is typically the hardest, most time consuming and costly stage. It is also the most fundamental and is vital to the success of the professional service firm. Planning marketing programmes, strategies and communications campaigns without rigorous, systematic market analysis will diminish the effectiveness of the firm's marketing effort and the use of its marketing resources by orders of magnitude. Some of the more mechanical and methodological issues in the collection of marketing information for market analysis will be dealt with in the following chapter in this section.

References

1 Wittreich, W. J. (1966), 'How to buy/sell professional services', *Harvard Business Review*, March/April, pp. 127–138.
2 Robinson, P. J., Faris C. W. and Wind Y. (1967), *Industrial Buying and Creative Marketing*, Boston: Allyn & Bacon.
3 Wind, Y. and Thomas, R. J. (1981), 'Conceptual and methodological issues in organisational buying behaviour', *European Journal of Marketing*, vol. 14, no. 5/6, pp. 239–247.
4 Webster, F. E. and Wind, Y. (1972), 'A general model of understanding buying behaviour', *Journal of Marketing*, vol. 36, April, pp. 12–19.
5 Lynn, S. A. (1987), 'Identifying buying influences for a professional service: implications for marketing efforts', *Industrial Marketing Management*, vol. 16, no. 2, pp. 119–30.
6 Tyebjee, T. T. and Bruno, A. V. (1982), 'Developing the marketing concept in public accounting firms', *Journal of the Academy of Marketing Science*, vol. 10, Spring, pp. 165–188.
7 George W. R. and Solomon, P. J. (1980), 'Marketing strategies for improved practice development', *The Journal of Accountancy*, (US), February, pp. 79–84.
8 Morgan, N. A. (1991), *Client Evaluations of Corporate Legal Advice*, SIMRU working paper, Cardiff Business School
9 Sarkar, A. K. and Saleh, F. A. (1974), 'The buyer of professional services: an examination of some key variables in the selection process', *Journal of Purchasing*, February, pp. 22–32.
10 Wheiler, K. (1987), 'Referrals between professional service providers', *Industrial Marketing Management*, vol. 16, pp. 191–200.
11 Howard, J. A. and Sheth, J. N. (1969), *The Theory of Buyer Behaviour*, New York: Wiley.
12 Hughes, M. A. and Kasulis, J. J. (1981), 'The production cue hypothesis and the marketing of legal services' in Bloch T., Upah, G. and Zeithaml, V. (eds), *Services Marketing in a Changing Environment*, Chicago: AMA.

4 Marketing information and research

Marketing information and research, despite the popular typology that exists in the UK, has very little to do with ladies in raincoats and clipboards on the local high street on a Saturday morning. This typology is probably less true in the professional service context than practically any other. In fact, while widespread confusion and uncertainty surround the whole area of marketing information and research, relatively simple and straightforward definitions and frameworks are available.

Marketing information is any information that may be useful as an input into the decision-making process in the marketing area. Thus a firm does not have to possess a formally organized marketing department in order to generate and make use of marketing information. Firms that do not formally organize marketing will still make decisions that may be seen to be 'marketing' decisions and will still therefore need marketing information if they are to make informed decisions. The types of 'marketing' decisions that one would expect to find being addressed by partners and practice managers are demonstrated in Figure 4.1.

Marketing strategy decisions	
Defining what business the firm is in – the mission	
Choosing service markets	
Choosing growth options	
Designing programmes for each mission area	
Marketing operations decisions	
Service/product	
policy	service development and selection, launches, modifications, branding
Pricing policy	fee levels, fee structures, quotations, discounts, fee packaging
Communications	advertising, budget, media, message, goals, promotion, budget, methods, goals
Distribution	office location, physical surroundings, service provider motivation, training communications

Figure 4.1 *Marketing decisions*

Within each of these marketing decision areas the decision type will

Table 4.1 *The management process*

Stage	Activities	Example
Analysis	Studying opportunities and competitors Making forecasts	There is a large demand in our area for construction projects. This market is worth £X and is growing at Y% per year.
Planning	Setting objectives and defining tasks and responsibilities	We want to gain 28 per cent of this market by developing a service offering through our project management department.
Implementation	Putting plans into action, getting resources, taking actions	Development of service with customer participation, free service trials, service is provided
Control	Evaluating actual achievements compared to plans & objectives, explaining variances	We got 5 per cent of the market worth £X at a cost of £Y; was analysis too optimistic? Was planning wrong? Did we fail to implement the plan properly? Are control measurements valid? Were there uncontrollable factors?

Adapted by the Author from Piercy and Evans (1983).[1]

be similar to those types of decisions that are made in all types of management.

Having defined what marketing information is, it may be useful at this stage to understand why marketing information is important in the professional service context.

The importance of marketing information

Information for decision making

Marketing information, i.e. information relating primarily to the firm's marketplace, its clients and competitors, obviously has an important role to play in practice management decision making. Given that management decision-making processes, and the 'quality' of practice management decisions are largely a product of the availability, type, timeliness and accuracy of information inputs, then the importance of marketing information is immediately obvious. While this may be logical and rational there is also evidence to suggest that many managers collect and use marketing information in order to justify actions already taken and decisions already made. Thus marketing information may be seen to have two uses in relation to decision making: (1) as an input to the decision-making process, a basis for defining options and choosing between them and (2) internally to reassure other managers, partners, etc. and 'sell' them a set of actions already taken and decisions already made.

Knowledge base for management

At a slightly deeper level we may see marketing information as an additional knowledge or database with which the PSF is managed. In the work of most professionals, technical knowledge and expertise in the specialist area of the relevant profession is constantly in use – indeed this is the basis of our service offering to clients. When professionals become involved in the management of a professional service firm, however, they require different types of knowledge and expertise. Contrary to the belief that seems to prevail in most professions, being a technically very good architect, lawyer, surveyor, accountant, doctor, etc., does not *necessarily* mean that the relevant professional will be successful in managing a professional service firm. Experience gained in their professional work is not often a sufficient knowledge base from which to become a practice manager involved in general management.[2] Marketing information can and does provide an additional or even alternative knowledge base for practice management which is immediately relevant since all management decisions will eventually impact upon the marketplace and the firm's clients – those who pay fees and determine the success of the firm.

Planning for the future

Having seen the importance of marketing information to the current management and decision-making activities within the firm, marketing information may be seen to have an even more important role in planning the future activities of the firm. The basis of any meaningful corporate or strategic plan is marketing information concerning clients, competitors and the marketplace. If a firm does not base its plans upon marketing information then it is usually unable to do anything more than react to changes in the environment as and when it becomes aware of them. In firms in which marketing information is not used such an awareness usually only emerges after environmental change has already impacted upon the firm's performance, i.e. something goes wrong and we try to find out why. The systematic collection and analysis of marketing information as a basis for practice planning will enable firms to adapt to market changes as they occur, and can often allow firms to anticipate changes and even 'control' or modify the changes that do occur in some cases.

There are therefore some very good reasons for recognizing that marketing information has an important role to play in the management and marketing of the professional service firm. It is necessary, however, to sound a note of caution at this point. In my experience I have often come across what I have called the 'information fallacy'. Many partners and managers use lack of marketing information as a reason for failing to make a concrete decision. Marketing information is obviously a vital input into management decision making as shown in Figure 4.2.

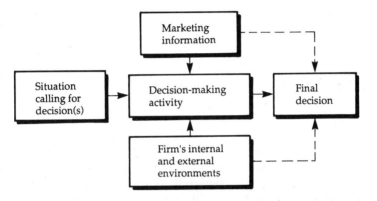

Figure 4.2 *Marketing information and decision making. Adapted from Parasuraman, A. (1986),* Marketing Research[3]

Decision makers cannot, however, expect marketing information to effectively make decisions for them. Marketing information must be seen as an aid to effective decision making and not a replacement for it. Partners and managers who wait for all the marketing information they feel they need to make a decision, will never make a decision at all, and in most cases such claims are merely an abdication of responsibility for making difficult and sometimes unpleasant decisions.

Within the professional service context there are two main sources of marketing information generation; marketing research and marketing intelligence, both of which cause problems for professionals and professional service firms. Both of these sources of marketing information are therefore worthy of closer examination.

Marketing research

Marketing research may be defined as a set of techniques and principles for systematically collecting, recording, analysing and interpreting data that can aid decision makers involved with the marketing of professional services. It is important to realize that marketing research is not simply the collection of data but more importantly the translation of information needs into the collection of relevant raw data which is then analysed and interpreted into marketing information in a format that fulfils the decision makers' information requirements.

There are a number of problems in the marketing research area in professional service firms that seem to crop up with alarming regularity; misinterpretation of decision makers' information needs, collecting information that's easily available rather than relevant, failing to analyse data properly, presenting results to decision makers in an inappropriate format, and an inability to use research agencies. All of these problems can be addressed, and to a large extent avoided, by taking a structured approach to planning a marketing research project.

Planning a research project

It is possible to take a structured approach to planning a marketing research project that can be applied as a framework each and every time marketing information is requested by decision makers or a marketing information need is identified within the firm. This framework can be broken down into a number of discrete stages that provide a systematic approach to planning marketing research.

1 *Define the brief* Crucial to the effectiveness and value of any research projects are the seemingly simple questions 'What do we need to find out?' and 'Why do we need this information?'. This stage of the planning framework may be seen to be the most important in determining the usefulness of the research to the firm. Without an accurate and adequate definition of what information is needed and for what purpose, all of the time, money and effort spent from that point on will be largely wasted and the firm's information needs will remain largely unfilled.

It is at this first stage that problems most frequently arise in using research agencies. I recently worked with a large law firm whose senior partner expressed heartfelt disillusionment with marketing research. Having decided that the firm lacked information concerning its clients' perceptions of its services the senior partner had invited proposals from six research agencies that had been recommended to him by commercial clients. After a meeting with each agency, written proposals were submitted. The senior partner found that the costs associated with each proposal varied widely, from £10,000 to over

£40,000. The approaches suggested by each firm in terms of what information to collect, from whom, and in what way varied even more widely. Given the law firm's inexperience in marketing research the senior partner felt unable to choose the 'right' proposal and thus the firm, even as I write, still lacks even basic marketing information. When I probed a little more deeply I discovered that the firm had at no time defined exactly what information they required and for what purpose. One would have hoped that in an ideal world the research agencies would have formulated such a brief with the firm. However, in the real world, in such a situation a large number of agencies would have merely designed their own brief, which best suited their own requirements, as they did in this case. The result in this particular example, however, was that the law firm never got the information it needed and none of the agencies picked up the assignment and a new client.

2 *Estimate the value* Before proceeding any further in putting together a research project it makes sense, once the brief has been sufficiently defined, to pose the obvious question, 'Is it worth it?'. While this seems a rather obvious question to ask it is surprising how many firms, once they have decided that obtaining marketing information is a good idea, commit themselves to a piece of market research without ever again asking themselves about the potential usefulness of the information they are seeking. This happens particularly in firms that have an approved marketing budget which will resource the research without further justification being needed from partnership committees, etc. Evaluating the potential usefulness of a research project is, however, difficult in itself. Obviously the potential usefulness depends upon the degree to which obtaining the marketing information sought will be helpful in making a particular decision and taking particular actions.

Estimating the value of marketing information is an inexact science. Professionals should, however, attempt to tackle this issue through a rudimentary cost–benefit approach.[4] The problems of using a cost–benefit approach will become immediately obvious to those involved. Estimating the costs of a research project is a relatively straightforward exercise, particularly if the firm has used research agencies or undertaken in-house research before. However, estimating the benefits that are likely to arise from a marketing research project in straight monetary terms is impossible. This side of the cost–benefit equation will, by necessity, be qualitative and largely a judgement call. In terms of evaluating benefits, even qualitatively, partners will need to evaluate at least two criterion: partnership attitudes and resource availability.

In terms of partnership attitudes, marketing research is only likely to be useful if partners and key decision makers are prepared to view the research with an open mind. I have found myself in the 'classic' position of presenting two research reports to an individual partner, the first of which confirmed ideas that the partner had about a particular marketplace and lent support to his embryonic plan for the firm to launch a new service. The second piece of research, however, highlighted problems with a market's awareness of both the firm and a particular service in an industrial sector following a marketing communication campaign, which the partner had personally planned. The partner accepted the first report with ill-concealed glee while rejecting the second report, claiming that he had 'suspected' the research methodology all along! This particular experience highlighted for me the necessity of relatively objective and open-minded users of marketing information. If you feel that the key decision-making partners in your firm are unlikely to accept and use marketing information in making decisions and taking actions then much of the potential benefits of a marketing research project may be lost.

In many cases, however, while decision-making partners are often not totally objective and open-minded in their use of marketing information, they may benefit from marketing research in a less tangible way. Even if the information obtained is not used specifically to make a particular decision one way or another, the information is often felt to be of value by partners as it can reduce their uncertainty about a particular decision area and can often give otherwise unavailable insights into a particular situation. In any cost–benefit analysis these dimensions of the value of marketing research should not be forgotten. Resource availability may also impinge upon the potential usefulness of a marketing research project. This is particularly likely to be true in research projects that are designed to uncover market opportunities. While marketing research is a good way to uncover such market opportunities and is often successful in doing so, the usefulness to the firm of the research will be greatly limited if the resources (e.g. budget, personnel, management time) are not available to make use of the information. It is possible for marketing research projects to be successful in terms of fulfilling their brief but for this information to be useless to the firm if it is not, or cannot be, used and acted upon in the way intended.

3   *Define specific data needs*   Having defined the brief in the first stage of planning a research project in terms of why information is required and what it will be used for, it is now necessary to turn the brief into a list of specific data that will satisfy the internal need for information. Often the purpose of the proposed research given in the brief can be

broken down into a number of constituent parts. It is necessary at this stage to define the specific data that will achieve each of the project's purposes. Most of the research projects that I have undertaken have, at this stage of planning, revealed a large number of different data requirements. A typical example was a brief received from a consulting engineering firm which wanted 'to determine our current market share and to ascertain what our relative market position is likely to be over the next two years'. This particular brief obviously required a number of different types of data in order to fulfil the firm's information needs, including:

- Market sizing of each of the markets in which the firm operated by service type.
- Determination of the firm's market share in each market from its revenue figures against the market sizings.
- Determination of market shares of major competitors in each service market.
- Degree of loyalty of clients to firm from turnover figures in client base, incorporating relative client importance.
- Trends in market share of major competitors in each service market over past years.
- Trends likely to affect total size of each of the service markets and forecasts of likely market size over a two-year period.

What may often seem a fairly obvious and sensible brief to a marketing partner or practice development committee is often found to be too large for a single marketing research project once the specific data needs have been established.

4   *Establish data sources*   Having defined specific data requirements it is obviously necessary to identify potential sources of these data. Data sources are usually classified by researchers as being either secondary or primary. Secondary data are relevant data that already exist, both inside and outside the firm, which have often been collected and collated for a different purpose. As secondary data is already in existence, although usually not in a suitable form for a particular research project, secondary research is a quick and cost-effective form of marketing research.

Internal secondary data such as the firm's own financial records, client files, old proposals and reports, etc. are almost always a necessary and fruitful data source in any research project. However, there is also a wealth of secondary data outside the firm that often remains under-utilized in most marketing research projects. These external secondary sources include: government departments, professional and trade bodies, published research (e.g. Mintel, EIU), universities, and even past reports, etc. from marketing research firms. PSFs should not under-estimate secondary research as an effective and relatively cheap way of fulfilling their marketing information needs. In the consulting engineers project, for example, at least some secondary data was necessary to fulfil each of the information requirements and was all that was necessary for some specific requirements such as market sizes and market share.

However, since secondary data was originally collected for other purposes it is necessary for researchers to check the relevance, impartiality and reliability of each source before incorporating it in any research project.

The alternative source of data is primary research. Primary data is original data obtained and produced to meet the specific data needs of the marketing research project being undertaken.

Since primary research involves generating new data from original sources it necessarily involves considerably more expertise, time, effort and budget than secondary research. There are usually three broad approaches to obtaining primary data: observation research, i.e. researchers simply watch and listen to clients as a professional service is delivered; survey research, the interactive questioning of clients, potential clients, referral sources, staff, etc. either by personal/group interview, telephone survey, or by written questionnaire; experimental research, consisting of giving selected matched groups different treatments, controlling for extraneous variables and checking differences between the groups.

5 *Design research methodology* This stage of planning a research project is most useful and most difficult when primary data is needed to fulfil the research brief and satisfy the project's specific data needs.

When primary data is required by a project then in most professional service cases a survey approach is the most applicable. At this stage of planning the research project we are primarily concerned with designing the instrument that will be used to elicit the required information from the sample. Many partners and professionals take an overly simplistic view of survey research and I have witnessed the results of projects where partners have decided that survey research is a simple case of asking a few obvious questions of a number of people in the target market. The results invariably indicate that questions have been asked either on the wrong issues or have been designed so badly that they do not elicit reliable responses. I also usually find that survey research conducted in-house by non-marketers produces more 'wouldn't it be nice to know if. . . ?' questions and results than critical 'need to know' findings. Partners will also try to sell their firm during data collection – this will only produce poor research and usually erodes the firm's image.

The areas that are important to examine and plan at this stage of the project include:

- At this stage do we need further qualitative information from interviews and focus groups or can we proceed, and do we need to conduct more formal quantitative research, sampling a larger number of people with a more formal survey instrument?
- How should the research questionnaire be approached? What types of questions are appropriate: open-ended, closed, multiple-choice, Likert scale, semantic differential, etc?
- What is the appropriate choice of words and sequences of questions in the questionnaire – can we pre-test the questionnaire on a pilot sample?
- What is the most appropriate means of collecting the data: personal interview, telephone interview or written postal questionnaire?

A cursory glance at these issues that need to be addressed for each research project in designing the research methodology suggests that a non-marketing professional is unlikely to have sufficient expertise and experience to undertake this stage of planning a marketing research project successfully. If at no other stage in a research project, professionals will need to seek advice in designing a research methodology which is going to be different for each individual research project.

6 *Design sample* An integral part of the research methodology is the sample design. The sample is simply those individuals and organizations selected as targets for the firm's effort to obtain primary information, i.e. those individuals that you interview or organizations to whom you send a questionnaire. The sample design stage involves three main decisions:

(a) What is the appropriate sampling unit, i.e. who precisely is the right kind of person or type of organization to survey. In most professional services marketing research the question is often more difficult in terms of commercial clients, i.e. in researching reasons for selecting a professional service firm should we be seeking answers to questions from users, influencers, buyers, deciders, etc. The answer to this question is far from obvious in most cases.

(b) How many units should be in the sample? In most cases it is not possible, or even necessary, to survey the whole of a population, whether that population is all the banks in the UK or the total number of home-owners. In general, however, the larger the sample size, the greater the number of responses and the greater the confidence in the research results.

(c) How should the sample be constructed? In these terms market researchers usually worry about constructing a random sample so that likely sampling errors can be excluded from the results. In my experience, more important at this stage with professional service firms is the construction of an objective and unbiased sample. Typically, surveying existing clients from a sample that is drawn 'in-house' by partners, etc., can produce incredibly biased results. This is unsurprising if one stops to think about it. Asking the heads of departments within a PSF for the names and addresses of twenty-five large, medium and small clients for a client satisfaction survey is likely to result in partners presenting samples for their department which contain those clients that they know well, drink with and even went to school with, so that the results for their department will look good within the firm. Objectivity in sample selection is vital.

7 *Collect data* At this stage the research project is actually implemented. The research instrument and design is used with the sample selected in the proceeding stages. In practically all projects data will also be collected at this stage from secondary sources which may be used as information to fulfil the brief and specific information needs identified in earlier stages of the research planning process. The major difficulties in this area are logistical in terms of the time, effort and cost of physically collecting the necessary raw data and in primary research in obtaining sufficient responses from the sample selected.

8 *Analyse and interpret data* The data collected above will, in its raw form, be largely useless in terms of fulfilling the organization's specific information needs. In this sense data is only useful to decision makers once it has been analysed and interpreted with the decision makers' specific needs in mind. The depth and degree of complexity of the analysis performed will obviously vary a great deal dependent upon the particular research project. PSFs should not underestimate the time and effort that may be required to analyse and interpret the results of a research project.

9 *Present research findings* Finally the results of the marketing research project need to fulfil their *raison d'être* by communicating the information required to the target audience. Typically this final stage of the project is the most rushed phase in PSFs. Partners and managers

who commissioned the project and funded it, whether in-house or externally, are often so anxious for results that they hope will at least appear to vindicate the budget spent in collecting them, that they rush the final presentation of the results and often minimize the potential impact upon decision makers within the firm.

Research findings do not have to be endless lists of tables and frequency responses and if presented in this way the potential value of research is often minimized by failing to attract the interest of decision makers that make up its audience. As a rough guide research findings should be presented in a concise and clearly structured form using graphic representation of quantitative findings where necessary. In the main report, pages of tables of statistical information should be avoided completely or alternatively added at the end of the report as an appendix for those who are interested. A one page general summary at the beginning is often a good idea and is appreciated by those within the firm who are not strictly in the target audience. Many firms also ignore oral presentation of the results to groups of partners, managers and other personnel, which can prove to be a powerful way of stimulating discussion and constructive response to research findings.

Using marketing research agencies

Most professional service firms in the UK do not have marketing research departments. Indeed many firms do not even have marketing departments or employ professional marketers. In such a position PSFs need to recognize their own limitations in terms of their ability to carry out marketing research in-house. However, given the relatively 'new' nature of marketing research needs in the service sector in general and the professional services sector in particular, few market- ing research agencies have had much experience in dealing with the marketing information problems and needs of professional service firms. In such relatively 'new' situations research agencies can often fall back upon information problem solutions that they are used to and have successfully used in FMCG sectors. This fails to address the very different information problems and needs of partners, professional marketers and managers in PSFs. The most critical stages of a research project are the writing of the brief and the definition of specific data needs. Most PSFs will experience some difficulty in objectively turning their internal decision-making problems into specific information needs. At this point it may be useful to ask a number of research agencies to prepare a proposal for your firm following a brief discussion. This will enable the firm (1) to get a better idea of its own information needs from the various proposals, and (2) to choose a potential supplier of marketing research services. This choice is usually made upon a research agency's ability to understand the PSF's problem rather than upon reputation, fees, etc. Having chosen a marketing research agency the PSF will then need to further discuss and refine the brief and specific information requirements (with the contents of the proposals received from other firms in mind) with the agency.

Current status of marketing research in PSFs

While it is relatively easy to demonstrate the need for and potential benefits of marketing information in professional service firms, one cannot escape the reality of the current status of marketing information and its allied activities within professional service firms in the UK. My own research has found that attitudes towards marketing research in the UK professional service firms are myopic and unenlightened.[5] The majority of firms in the accounting, legal and engineering professions do not buy even syndicated or published research when it is available, let alone commission original research from outside specialists. While the majority of firms in all three professions claim to recognize a need for marketing research in their firms, most attempt to fulfil this need in-house, usually with inexperienced and unqualified personnel, in an unstructured, informal way.

Given this prevailing attitude towards the importance of marketing information and activities within professional service firms the research into the level of use of types of marketing research that are most applicable to the professions produced unsurprising results. An example from the law firm studies is shown in Table 4.4.[6]

Table 4.4 *Types of marketing research undertaken*

Activities	Level of use		
	Frequently (%)	Sometimes (%)	Never (%)
Market potential – existing offices	14	39	47
Market potential – new offices	5	41	54
Market share analysis	12	26	62
Market characteristics	16	30	54
Customer characteristics	19	32	49
Advertising effectiveness	14	26	60
Advertising media research	9	26	65
Advertising copy research	8	18	74
New service potential	4	35	61
Competitor studies	18	32	50
Pricing studies business trends	12	37	51

Although the relative importance of activities varies in the accountancy and consulting engineering studies the overall level of marketing research activities remains low.[7]

Since a firm cannot begin to really become a client-centred, market-oriented business without undertaking some form of marketing research to identify specifically, and in detail, exactly what client needs are, then the attitude of PSFs toward marketing information and the level of use of marketing research both need to be changed dramatically.

Market(ing) intelligence

While marketing research is a fundamental and necessary activity if a firm is to become market oriented it is not in itself sufficient to ensure that the firm knows and fulfils its clients' needs. Many of the problems faced by professional service firms in the UK over the last decade have resulted from the degree and rate of change in the markets and business environments in which they operate.

Marketing research can provide specific information upon client needs, attitudes, etc. However, if a firm wishes to be truly market oriented and effective in its competitive marketing efforts, then it needs to be able to anticipate client needs and attitudes in order to be able to adjust its marketing mix accordingly. While forecasting of any kind is notoriously difficult, the complexity and rapidity of change which has characterized the business environment of both PSFs and their clients for the past decade necessitate systematic and rigorous analysis of the firm's business and marketing environment as an integral part of its business and marketing planning efforts.

While many firms recognize the validity of this argument they quite rightly counter with 'so, what can we do about it?'. Most firms do already undertake informal 'undirected viewing', i.e. the partners and staff of the firm will read the professional magazines and journals in an attempt to keep up with changes within the profession and the activities of competitors, etc. While this may be useful, it frequently yields information that is too 'old' to be of competitive and marketing use.

What prevents most firms from going further than this in their environmental scanning efforts is the lack of a framework to use in studying what is, after all, a huge and complex business environment. We can be of some help in providing a framework with which to analyse the business environment. First, we can break down the entire environment into a number of relatively discrete areas for analysis. These major areas of environmental analysis are:

65

1 *Legal and political change*
   What are likely to be the ongoing effects of existing legislation? What new legislation is likely to be introduced? Is there likely to be a change in government and what might this mean? What changes are likely in the next budget? What aspects of Europe-wide legislation are likely to be important to this firm and its clients?

2 *Economic change*
   What is likely to happen to exchange rates and interest rates? What effects will expansion or recession have? How are the economics of the labour market likely to change? What effects will inflation have upon our investment in the firm?

3 *Technological developments and change*
   How will technology change client needs and expectations? How will technology change the way we produce and distribute our services? What administrative and management benefits are we likely to derive from technology and how will this impact on our cost structure? In what ways will technology affect the way our clients do business?

4 *Cultural and social change*
   How will population growth affect our markets and their needs? What will be the effect of the 'greying' of the population upon clients and us? In what ways will personal and corporate relocation affect our clients and us? What changes in the way society views business are likely and how will this affect our clients and our own firm?

5 *Institutional change*
   Will the nature of the traditional institutions in our marketplace change? How are the structures of the markets in which we operate likely to change? In what ways are channels of distribution changing for our clients and how might this affect us? What changes are likely in professional regulation and how may these affect us?

6 *External competitor developments*
   What developments are likely to occur with our existing major competitors? What new competitors are likely to enter the market-place? Is there a threat of new competition from outside the marketplace in terms of generic competitors? Are we likely to encounter foreign competition?

This framework can be used by professional service firms to focus their identification of relevant environmental moves and assess the areas in which the firm needs to collect and analyse information. Under each of the areas of the environment identified above there are a number of specific questions that need to be addressed within the firm:

1   In each area what changes or events can we envisage?
2   In what way would these events or changes impact upon our firm in terms of the way that we interact with and service our clients?
3   Would these changes/events be beneficial to our firm and our clients, or harmful?
4   How likely are these events/changes to happen?
5   How will these changes/events affect our major competitors and what is their likely reaction?

At this stage of environmental scanning we have identified the relevant issues arising from the marketing environment, assessed the nature and scope of their implications for the firm and the likelihood of these environmental changes occurring. This will generate valuable information and insights which will form an integral part of the marketing and business planning within the firm.

Perhaps more importantly this framework operates as a scanning device which is useful in a number of other ways. First, identifying issues which have been found to be potentially important to the firm but about which partners and those responsible for marketing and planning in the firm have little information. Thus the screening process identifies critical issues and areas in which the firm may not only need to gather and analyse further information, but which may be deemed to be important enough to monitor on a systematic and on-going basis. Second, having identified issues and events through the scanning process, it is possible to consider how the firm can negate, lessen or even alter the likely impact of environmental changes upon the firm. Alternatively, with events and changes that are beneficial, can the firm either increase the likelihood of these events occurring or increase the beneficial effects that they might have upon the firm?

This simple framework can be adapted and developed into a systematic, structured, worksheet-driven process which can become an integral part of the firm's strategic and marketing planning efforts.

Marketing information systems

An increasing number of professional service firms are now beginning to integrate their marketing information activities into formal computer-based marketing information systems. While establishing a formal marketing information system may sound like a daunting, complex and expensive task this need not necessarily be the case.

A marketing information system is simply a formal system of collecting, organizing, analysing and reporting information that may be useful in making marketing and strategic decisions as shown in Figure 4.3.

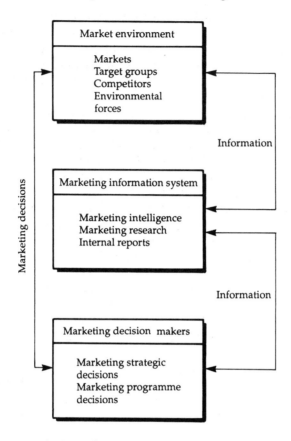

Figure 4.3 *Marketing information system (MKiS)*

Professional service firms considering introducing a formal marketing information system must beware of falling into the technology
'trap'. While most MKiSs will in the 1990s be computer-based, the
effectiveness in use of MKiSs has little to do with the computing
hardware and software involved. Indeed many MKiSs are under-used
and ineffective because they are designed and developed by computer
and systems experts rather than management decision makers.
Effective MKiSs have to be designed from the user's perspective if they
are to be anything more than expensive and little used technological
toys. Essentially the goal of most MKiSs is to develop a database of all
of the firm's marketing information in a system that can analyse the
data and present the information required by the user in a useful
format for marketing decision making.

The obvious starting point in achieving this goal is the definition of
the information needs and requirements of the user. Determining the

marketing information needs of partners and managers is, however, a problematic task for a number of reasons; partners and managers often claim that they already are presented with too much information, and predicting marketing information needs can be difficult since decision makers often don't know what information they will need (Piercy and Evans, 1983).[8] Clearly, given such constraints and difficulties in assessing marketing information needs when designing an MKiS, firms are unlikely to be able to establish a system that will exactly meet their unfolding decision-making information needs. However, when establishing an MKiS, a firm needs to start somewhere in terms of defining information needs. In most cases this can simply be achieved through an internal questionnaire of all those involved in strategic and marketing decisions. Such a questionnaire is usually best used via personal interviews. Questions would normally cover the following areas:

- Types of decisions involved with on a frequent basis.
- Information currently used in making these decisions.
- Information currently received on a regular basis.
- Information obtained infrequently.
- Perceived information gaps.

This will *not* produce a perfect and exhaustive list of information that, if provided, would be extensively used in strategic and marketing decision making. It will, however, produce a rough outline of the sorts of information which, if provided, partners and managers might find useful.

Professional service firms need to view an MKiS as a developing decision support system which will be constantly amended, updated and developed both to better serve decision makers' existing information needs and to keep pace with their changing information needs in the future. An important point allied to this is that in establishing an MKiS a firm needs to effectively communicate this message to those who are likely to be users. Raising high expectations of a new MKiS is likely to seriously diminish users' perceptions of the MKiS in the initial stages which can diminish utilization for a considerable period of time in some cases.

Indeed in establishing a marketing information system both PSFs and likely MKiS users need to be made aware of the limitations of MKiSs such as: an MKiS cannot replace managerial judgement, it cannot provide all the information that a decision maker would need to make infallible decisions, and it cannot serve and fulfil a useful function unless it is constantly developed and enhanced in terms of meeting user information needs.

Database marketing

One specific aspect of marketing information systems that is being heavily 'sold' into professional service firms by outside consultants is database marketing. There appears to be something of a 'panacea' image that has rapidly become associated with database marketing and many firms that are appointing an in-house marketing professional for the first time are asking for marketing databases to be built before any other marketing activities are undertaken.

While database marketing sounds like a scientific, technologically sophisticated and rigorous approach to marketing, the reality of such databases in most PSFs is that it is actually concerned essentially with what we have been happy to label, until now, mailing lists. It is simply the recording on a computer database of contact names, client and potential client addresses, previous contact with the firm and any details of client information and needs from client files. The rapid growth of database marketing as an approach in the UK has basically followed the trend towards direct mail as a marketing communications medium and has been particularly important in building the financial services 'junk mail' marketing culture.

Proponents of database marketing see two major advantages from its approach:

(a) It enables marketers to specifically target their marketing communications activities thus increasing the effectiveness of budget spent.
(b) Databases can be used to test communications campaigns, fee changes, new services, etc.

While the first of these advantages may well have some basis in reality, the level of use of direct mail and telemarketing in most professional service firms is not of a sufficient size and scale to warrant a full-blown database. The second strength of database marketing effectively does nothing more than provide a sampling frame for marketing research. It gives no more aid to the decision maker than producing a list of clients, etc. that they may seek specific marketing information from.

Database marketing can provide some benefits in sophisticated marketing environments in large companies. This does not, however, mean that it provides the answer to the marketing needs of marketing unsophisticated professional partnerships. PSFs should therefore beware of large investments in technology and consultancy in purchasing and establishing a marketing database and expecting this to solve the firm's marketing problems. In most cases the potential and realized benefits of marketing databases in professional service firms do not justify the investment in them.

References

1 Piercy, N. and Evans, M. (1983), *Managing Marketing Information*, London: Croom Helm.

2 Lorsch, J. W. and Mathias, P. E. (1987), 'When professionals have to manage', *Harvard Business Review*, July/August, pp. 78–83.

3 Parasuraman, A. (1986), *Marketing Research*, Reading, Mass: Addison Wesley.

4 Morgan, N. A. (1988), 'Marketing information and professional service firms', *Professional Practice Management*, vol. 7, no. 1, pp. 8–10.

5 Morgan, N. A. (1990), 'Marketing in UK accounting firms', *The Service Industries Journal*, vol. 10 no. 3, July

6 Morgan, N. A. (1989), *Marketing in UK Law Firms*, University of Wales Cardiff Business School working paper in marketing and strategy.

7 Morgan, R. and Morgan, N. A. (1990), *Marketing Consulting Engineering Services*, Cardiff Business School, SIMRU working paper.

8 Piercy, N. and Evans, M., op. cit.

Part Three
Strategic Marketing Planning

Professional service firms seem to have a good deal of difficulty with marketing at the strategic level in terms of creating marketing strategies and developing strategic marketing plans. Most of the explicit strategies and formal strategic marketing plans that I see in PSFs are basically either communications plans and/or extended budget requests – there is nothing that may be considered to be strategic about them other than the use of the word 'strategic' often in gold block letters on the cover of the written plan or document. In many firms these 'plans' and 'strategies' represent little more than last year's 'plan' or 'strategy' with figures adjusted for inflation.

In delving deeper into this problem in PSFs it becomes evident that most firms differentiate between marketing plans and strategies, and 'corporate' or 'business' plans and strategies. This does not solve the initial problem, however, since few firms seem to have explicit corporate or business plans either. There is really no distinction between corporate and business plans and strategic marketing plans and strategies in the 'real' world. The differences are almost wholly semantic and both should be addressing the same issues and from the same perspective.

There are a number of readily identifiable problems that most PSFs encounter in strategic marketing planning. The most obvious are concerned with:

- Setting strategic goals and directing the firm's efforts.
- Focusing upon identifiable market segments and target markets.
- Achieving a competitive differentiation in service marketplaces.
- Identifying and analysing competitors.
- Developing a strategic marketing planning process.
- Getting marketing plans and strategies actually implemented.

This section of the book directly addresses all of these major problem areas (plus a few others as well!). Chapter 5 opens up the whole issue of strategic perspective and the elements of marketing strategies that are commonly developed by professional service firms. The following chapters look internally at identifying strategic direction, goals and objectives, the tools and techniques available for strategic planning, the issues to be addressed in the strategic audit, choosing between alternative strategy options, etc. Externally, the chapters focus upon market segmentation and target marketing, identifying and analysing competition and developing a competitive differentiation which can be delivered into the marketplace.

5 Strategic marketing of professional services

Marketing strategy

The term marketing strategy is used widely and very loosely in the professional service arena, being applied to anything from an analytical and detailed marketing plan for a national firm to the proposal for a new 'corporate image' by a design company. Ambiguity and uncertainty about precise definitions of strategic marketing and marketing strategy (these terms are widely interchangeable) abound even amongst the world's leading academics, consultants and practitioners.

In order to try to avoid such ambiguity in the minds of the reader I propose a 'working' definition for the purposes of this section of the book:

> Strategic marketing is the management process of developing and implementing a planned approach to the way in which the firm can best service its chosen target markets and achieve its long-term goals.

Thus, in crude terms, strategic marketing is concerned with the 'what' of the organization's direction rather than the specific 'how' of getting there. While defining exactly what is, and ought, to be implied by 'strategic marketing' is difficult there are a number of characteristics which differentiate between strategic and tactical levels.

Strategic marketing is long range: the decisions involved in strategic marketing have long-term implications for the firm. They are not concerned with the day-to-day decisions which have relevance only over a few months. Strategic marketing plans have time-scales in years rather than months.

Strategic marketing is a senior management responsibility: while the specifics of producing a new brochure for a particular service are typically left in most PSFs to the marketing manager or delegated to an assistant, developing and implementing a marketing strategy has such wide-ranging implications for the future of the firm that it typically involves senior level managers and partners.

Strategic marketing accepts no constraints: strategic marketing questions the assumptions that PSFs make about markets, competitors, clients and the firm, and seeks to redefine the firm's mission, approach and actions in this arena. Marketing programmes and tactics, on the other hand, accept the status-quo and work within that to achieve limited specified goals.

Strategic marketing deals with the whole organization: while marketing programmes and tactics are concerned with individual services or individual markets, even individual clients, strategic marketing is concerned with the whole of an organization and how it might best relate to its environment.

Importance of strategic perspective

There are a number of very good reasons for adopting a strategic perspective in marketing professional services:

Pro-active vs reactive firms: the marketing activities of most professional service firms take place at a tactical level and are largely reactive in terms of existing client needs, current market conditions and recent competitor activities. Thus, given the dynamic nature of the business environment facing PSFs in the 1990s and the increasing rapidity of environmental change, most of the marketing activities of PSFs are based on historical information and are 'out of date' as soon as they are undertaken.

In most cases the marketing research and intelligence activities of firms are insufficient for even reasonably rapid reaction to changes in the environment and firms often fail to become aware of the existence and significance of changes in markets, clients, competitors, technology, etc. until their own financial performance is affected to a sufficient extent to make partners ask questions.

Strategic marketing is essentially about creating pro-active PSFs that anticipate environmental change and plan marketing tactics and programmes accordingly. In some cases it is even possible to influence potential environmental change in the firm's own interest or at least to have the opportunity to plan the best way to respond and prepare for anticipated change. Designing marketing programmes and tactics that reflect the existing marketplace, current client needs and historical competitor thrusts may have been sufficient for survival in the 1980s. Survival in the 1990s requires much more, it requires pro-active marketing planning, it requires *strategic* marketing.

Direction and focus: approaching the marketing of professional services as a set of projects that are discrete and independent is a waste of resources in the long term. What a strategic perspective brings to marketing is a direction and focus to the diverse marketing activities undertaken within the firm. Strategic marketing is not about achieving maximum efficiency in the use of the marketing budget of the firm. It is about achieving the most effective allocation of all of the firm's resources (including human resources) in chosen target markets.

Most of the activities of both marketers and professionals in professional service marketing lack the coherence that a strategic perspective brings. If we believe that all client contact and service provision personnel are involved in our firm's marketing efforts then we need to be able to demonstrate a focused, consistent direction that we wish them to take. This is almost impossible to do without taking a strategic marketing approach to the planning of the firm's marketing efforts.

Client orientation: as we saw in Chapter 1 the achievement of a client orientation is one of the key goals of marketing in professional service firms. Reaching this marketing goal within the firm is seldom easy and the functional isolation of marketing that exists in most firms makes this even more difficult. Strategic marketing has an important role to play in moving the firm towards a client orientation by questioning the assumption that partners actually know why clients choose one firm rather than another and what their real professional service needs actually are, and involving partners in the development of the strategic marketing plan.

The adoption of a strategic marketing approach in the professional service context is most readily operationalized via a structured and systematic strategic marketing planning process.

If the adoption of a strategic marketing perspective can potentially achieve all of the above benefits in a professional service firm then why hasn't everybody developed and implemented a strategic marketing planning process?

This is a very good question. It is also a question that I cannot personally answer since failing to implement even a rudimentary marketing planning process seems to me to be tantamount to gross professional negligence. I have, however, posed this very question to both partners and professional marketers in a large number of professional service firms, of all sizes, all over the country. Most of the reasons given for not developing a strategic marketing planning process are rooted in the way in which professional service firms were able to survive and even prosper in the 1960s and 1970s with relatively stable business environments. Thus partners make comments such as 'we have been a well-known and profitable firm for the past twenty years without any marketing planning' and 'we provide the quality professional services that clients want. We do not need strategic marketing planning.'

From a slightly different angle some partners and senior managers see the development of strategic marketing planning as implying something of a failure on their part. One partner in an engineering firm responded to the question in a somewhat hostile tone 'I know this business like the back of my hand. I do not need to write it down.' It should be remembered that marketing planning, as a management activity, can create a good deal of discomfort amongst partners and senior managers simply by questioning assumptions that they and the firm unquestionably accept.

There are also a number of objections to marketing planning that are based upon marketing planning itself both as a management process and the plans and strategies and result. These objections usually relate to management time and effort 'marketing planning would take up too much of my time and I am a fee earner you know!', and the nature of planning itself 'marketing planning would discourage individual initiative' and 'plans are inflexible and our markets simply change too quickly'.

Implementation is also seen to be a critical area in views upon marketing planning and its potential usefulness in PSFs. Many partners and senior managers have commented upon the implementation of plans and strategies amongst their reasons for not developing marketing planning. This area causes particular concern amongst professional marketers. 'Marketing plans rarely came true, so why bother preparing them', 'Nobody ever uses them anyway' and 'It would merely be a meaningless ritual in this firm.'

Some sympathy must be expressed with some of the sentiments that partners and senior managers seem to hold in many PSFs that militate against strategic marketing planning. However, it must be said that all of these comments relate to poorly designed and badly implemented strategic marketing planning processes rather than strategic marketing planning *per se*.

The strategic marketing planning process

Strategic marketing planning is usually presented as a systematic flow model of the stages that it is necessary to go through in order to develop a strategic marketing plan. This is shown in Figure 5.1. This is also an indication of what normally needs to be included in a written marketing plan.

This section of the book deals with each of the stages in the marketing planning process, explaining and illustrating the tools,

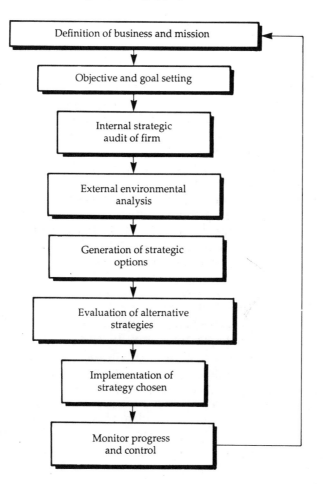

Figure 5.1 *Professional services marketing planning process*

techniques and frameworks that are available and how they may usefully be applied in the strategic marketing of professional services.

In purely rational terms, the creation and development of a well-researched and analysed written marketing plan obviously has a number of potential benefits for any professional service firm. It ensures that all the firm's strategic development is based upon its internal strengths and it forces a market focus into the firm's activities. In analysing client and market behaviour it allows early and systematic identification of potential market opportunities and thus ensures that the firm's resources are applied effectively in terms of longer-term development and growth and therefore leads to increases in fee income and ultimately profitability. While these potential benefits alone present a fairly strong case for developing a strategic marketing plan, these can be seen to be output benefits, i.e. benefits of possessing a 'good' marketing plan.

What are often neglected are the benefits of actually going through the process, i.e. the benefits of 'planning' as opposed to the benefits of the 'plan'. In professional practices in which I have been involved in developing and implementing a strategic marketing planning process, the partners of the firm often admit to benefiting more from going through the planning process than actually possessing and using the resulting plan. The particular 'planning' related benefits that are most often recognized by PSFs include: the development of new planning skills amongst partners and senior managers, the ongoing and continuous nature of the process instead of a 'once a year ritual', the involvement of partners in planning producing teams and the 'owner-ship' of plans, a mechanism for legitimate 'shaking the dogma' and challenging the existing 'mind-set' that is apparent in the best of PSFs let alone the worst, the identification of information needs and the use and sharing of relevant existing information within the firm, and in general a more confident attitude towards the future with a greater sense of common purpose and direction within the firm.

Examining the potential benefits of strategic marketing planning in this way illustrates that while the existence of a 'good' marketing plan is a prerequisite in the world of professional services marketing, simply getting a suitably qualified consultant or even your in-house marketing professional to write such a plan for your firm is not enough. The way in which the plan or strategy is developed and formulated has potentially an even greater benefit for the firm's strategic and marketing development than the simple possession of a strategic marketing plan.

Developing a marketing planning process

The vast majority of professional service firms in the UK, even some of the very biggest, have nothing even approaching a 'textbook' market-ing planning system or process. Given the potential process and content benefits that have been identified, many professional service firms may see the value of developing a marketing planning process – if they have some idea about where to start.

While this book is not designed to be a prescriptive 'how to' manual, it may be of value to many readers at this stage to make explicit what marketing planning 'should' be if it is to realize the potential process and content benefits associated with it. In these terms marketing planning should be:

Structured: i.e. it is no good simply requiring departmental heads or even marketing partners to produce a marketing plan. Non-professional marketers (and even some marketing professionals) will fail to prepare and develop a successful marketing plan unless they are given a structured framework within which to work. In most cases this means developing a rudimentary planning manual and giving partners and managers the necessary training and skills to use it.

Iterative: one of the key terms in the marketing planning process should be iteration; i.e. simply moving through the stages of planning until you reach the end is not enough. Effective planning necessitates moving backwards and forwards between the stages within the process, feeding the results of one piece of analysis back to the beginning or making one decision and seeing how that will affect everything else by working it back through the process. Iteration is a word that will be used often throughout this section of the book.

Market focus: the biggest part of any marketing plan and any strategic business plan is market analysis covering all of the areas such as sizing, buying behaviour, needs, factors influencing purchase decisions, etc. that were made explicit in the preceding section. Any strategic marketing planning process that doesn't focus upon the marketplace and client needs as the driving force behind successful and effective strategy formulation is likely to fail.

Make assumptions explicit: in any planning process it is necessary to make assumptions. In poor planning processes, however, strategic assumptions are made implicitly and are rarely questioned. If and when assumptions have to be made in planning then they need to be made explicitly and they need to be validated as much as possible. It is surprising how often firms carry assumptions forward in their planning year after year. When the assumption was originally made it may well have been valid – this is much less likely to be true five years later. All assumptions in planning need to be made explicit and need to be validated.

Participative: marketing planning at the strategic level is not something that only the marketing partners, practice development committee or marketing consultant does. There are two main issues here: (i) marketing planning cannot be undertaken by an individual, (ii) in terms of participation it makes a lot of sense to involve those who will be implementing the resulting plans and strategies.

Managed: while all the books and consultants will 'sell' professional service firms planning processes, not unlike the flow model of the planning process in this chapter, this is frequently not enough to ensure that planning 'happens' in the real world. My colleague Nigel Piercy and I have been working on this problem specifically over the last couple of years. The essential message of our work has been that in terms of implementation we have to view the strategic marketing planning process as having at least three dimensions.

Successful strategic marketing planning requires the consistent 'management' of these levels of planning process (Figure 5.2) and a recognition that techniques of analysis and formal planning procedures are not in themselves enough to ensure an effective marketing planning process. These issues will be expanded and discussed in the final section of this book.

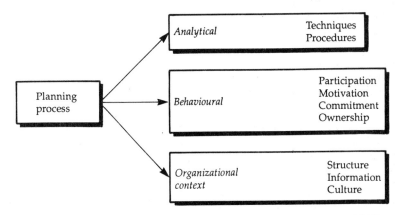

Figure 5.2 *Dimensions of planning process (Piercy and Morgan, 1990)*

Given such a 'shopping list' of requirements to be considered in developing a strategic marketing planning process it is obvious that such a planning system is only possible and effective in professional service firms that either possess or develop supportive organizational cultures. This will involve, at the very least, the removal of the active disincentives to marketing planning that exist in most professional service firms, e.g. training partners and managers in planning skills and giving them adequate time and resources for running planning teams and meetings. Simply asking partners and managers to undertake marketing planning, as well as all their other service provision and fee-earning tasks, does not serve to demonstrate the importance that the firm places upon planning strategies for the future. Similarly, evaluating and rewarding staff and partners for their short-term ability to secure fee income and technical competence does not motivate or encourage members of the firm to spend a good deal of their time and effort involved in longer-term, non-'billable' planning activities. If the firm wishes to have a 'strategic orientation' then it needs to evaluate planning skills and performance and reward them in the same way as fee-earning activities.

Much of the activity of building a supportive culture within a firm for strategic marketing is about the senior members of the partnership, i.e. those with the real power and 'clout' in the organization, sending signals through their actions and words that lead the rest of the firm to recognize that strategic marketing is important. Failure to do so leads to ritualistic 'once a year' planning that produces plans and strategies that rarely get implemented by the firm. A waste of time and effort that is recognized as such by those involved in the planning even if not by the senior management of the firm.

The following chapters in this section of the book outline and explain some of the major tools and techniques available to PSFs in formulating strategic marketing plans. However, there are a number of strategic marketing issues that are often not directly addressed by the traditional procedures involved in marketing planning and yet are critical to the development of a comprehensive and useful marketing plan. These issues include:

Competitive differentiation: given that in most professions the major PSF competitors in a marketplace offer largely generic services, then a critical component of any strategic marketing plan should be a consideration of how to achieve a service that is recognized by both existing and potential clients as being different from the service offerings of competitors, and ideally different in a way that clients not only recognize, but also value. For example, any consulting engineering firm could differentiate itself by sending its staff to sites wearing purple hard hats with pink spots on. This does not, however, differentiate their firm from its competitors on a basis that 'adds value' from the client's point of view. If, however, the firm differentiates itself by guaranteeing the client's timing schedule with self-imposed over-run penalties, then this certainly would differentiate the firm and on a basis that the client would not only recognize but value highly.

Sustainable comparative advantage: any marketing strategy for any PSF that is in any way in competition for clients and fee income will spend much of its strategic marketing efforts searching for internal capabilities, skills, resources, expertise, assets (both tangible and intangible), etc. that either already exist within the firm, or that potentially may be developed within the firm that will provide some advantage, either in terms of cost (internal not necessarily fee levels) or differentiation, over major competitors in the marketplace. A comparative advantage is often difficult to build, whatever its basis, and the investment of time and effort is only likely to pay off if the comparative advantage is capable of being protected and is difficult for competitors to copy or evaluate.

Implementation: any strategic marketing plan or strategy proposal that does not contain explicitly and in detail, with cost implications, an implementation strategy within it should be bounced straight back to the team or group that formulated it. In the relatively few PSFs that do develop marketing and business strategies and plans, most of them fail to achieve the implementation of their plans and strategies to anything like the degree that was envisaged. We shall return to this issue as one of fundamental importance to achieving the implementation of the marketing concept, in the final section of the book.

The reality of PSF strategic marketing

Through my various research activities and consultancy work with PSFs in the UK, the reality of strategic marketing across all professions is that marketing is seen very much as a support service with no special input into the strategic planning and direction of the firm. Indeed in most of the research the marketing function has less of a role in strategic and corporate planning than the other critical functional areas of finance and personnel. As was shown in Chapter 2 the input of marketing to other 'strategic' activities such as diversification planning and fee income forecasting is even less than in strategic planning.

The harsh reality is that in most firms marketing is seen overwhelmingly as a tactical activity with responsibility for running marketing programmes, primarily communications programmes. In most PSFs, large and small, irrespective of profession there exists nothing that even vaguely resembles a strategic marketing planning process. Where firms do claim to have a structured, strategic approach to marketing they are normally talking about producing a strategic marketing plan that is essentially a series of extended budgets and income forecasts.

While the development of a strategic marketing planning process is obviously a fundamental foundation for all of the firms marketing and corporate development, and the lack of the firms marketing and corporate development, and the lack of a strategic approach to marketing in most PSFs is increasingly evident, it should also be noted that in UK industry as a whole estimates of companies that do undertake a structured strategic marketing planning process range between 10 and 20 per cent. However, simply claiming that 'we are no worse than anyone else' in respect of strategic marketing is hardly a credible defence for UK PSFs. If anything, the failure of most firms to realize the benefits of a strategic marketing planning process presents an opportunity for other firms to make headway against competitors.

As one part of the exploratory research into marketing in the accounting, legal and consulting engineering professions we attempted to get some idea of the perceived 'critical success factors' in the marketing strategies adopted by firms. This was done simply by presenting those responsible for a firm's marketing with a list of the elements normally found in the marketing strategies of PSFs and asking them to score each element in terms of its relative importance within their own marketing strategy.

This produced a view of the critical elements in marketing strategy in PSFs which was very similar in all three professions. The results of the study of consulting engineers (Table 5.1)[2] were remarkably similar to those found in the accounting and legal professions.

Table 5.1 *Consulting engineers – elements in marketing strategy*

	Very important (%)	Mean (5 = very important) score (1 = no importance)
Professional reputation	92	4.9
Technical service excellence	88	4.9
Image of firm	81	4.8
Specialist services for defined segment	41	4.6
Personal contacts of staff	61	4.5
Utilization of technology	46	4.4
Level of fees	50	4.3
Range of services provided	39	4.2
Social contacts of staff	29	3.8
Promotional literature	22	3.6
Location and distribution of firm's offices	17	3.5
Advertising	0	2.4

The view of marketing strategies adopted by UK PSFs is interesting in that it raises a number of very obvious questions, most of which I have already posed to those with marketing responsibilities in PSFs all over the country, and to which I have yet to achieve satisfactory answers from those same people.

The critical elements found in all of the professions studied are professional reputation and technical service excellence. Both elements, by their very nature, are intangible. In most firms there exists a widespread belief that professional reputation is essentially a product of the technical abilities of the firm's personnel in their area of expertise. The obvious question, that has yet to be considered in many firms, is 'how can anyone who has not experienced our service evaluate our technical expertise'. This is a particularly pertinent question in a number of respects; how is technical service excellence communicated to those potential clients that have yet to experience it first hand, particularly since the communications elements of promotion and advertising are seen as the least important elements in most firms' marketing strategies. Similarly there is an assumption in most PSFs that clients judge the firm upon its technical ability when in reality most clients are not confident or competent enough to even attempt to evaluate the firm's technical service offering.

Solving these problems is not easy. The problems associated with communicating intangible benefits to both existing and potential clients are largely intactable and will be examined further in Part Four of this book. However, it is evident that the marketing strategies currently adopted by most PSFs pose significant problems if they are to be successfully implemented, and make assumptions that may be difficult, if not impossible, to validate.

References

1 Piercy, N. and Morgan, N. (1990), 'Internal marketing strategy as a lever for market-led strategic change,' *Irish Marketing Review*, vol. 4, no. 3, pp. 11–29.
2 Morgan R. and Morgan, N. (1991), 'An exploratory study of marketing orientation in the UK consulting engineering profession', *Journal of Advertising*, vol. 10, Autumn.

6 Developing a strategic marketing plan

Having discussed the need for PSFs to adopt a strategic perspective in their marketing activities and the potential benefit to firms of developing a systematic strategic marketing planning process and documented marketing plans, this chapter focuses upon *what* needs to be considered in a marketing planning exercise and *how* strategic issues can usefully be analysed using some of the tools and techniques that have been developed by academics and consultants.

Mission analysis

Most of the 'classical' marketing planning processes proposed and developed by consultants and academics begin with the development for the firm of a 'mission' or 'vision' statement. Such statements usually attempt to capture and communicate the *'raison d'être'* of the firm, providing a focus and 'common thread' for the activities of the firm.

This idea of defining the mission of a business grew from the classic 1960 article by Theodore Levitt of the Harvard Business School in which he described how many American companies, by defining their business activities in terms of their product or service offering, had artificially limited their perspective upon potential areas of growth and potential 'generic' competitors.[1] This was implicitly recognized by accountancy firms in the 1970s when mission statements began to be developed that talked about providing 'business solutions' rather than 'accounting services'. This redefinition of the business based upon the customer need rather than the existing service offering allowed the accountancy firms to enter other facets of 'business solutions' provision in areas as diverse as IT consultancy, recruitment and selection services and corporate relocation services. This customer-needs definition not only allowed accountancy firms to grow their businesses in a series of areas that were growing far more rapidly than the market for auditing and taxation advice but brought an awareness that, as well as facing traditional competitors in terms of other accountancy firms, they were also facing competition from 'generic' competitors from sources as diverse as merchant banks, computer manufacturers, software houses, management consultancies, estate agencies and even universities. Thus competitive strategies and positioning need to be considered not only in terms of how to find comparative advantage and competitive differentiation in terms of positioning *vis-à-vis* other accountancy firms, as had traditionally been the case, but also *vis-à-vis* all of the new 'generic' competitors in each marketplace.

In these terms mission analysis is simply a case of answering four basic questions:

1 *What business are we in?*
   This question is initially tackled by most firms in terms of their own service offerings or technology along the lines of 'we are in the law business' or 'the civil engineering business'. Such answers and approaches are unlikely to produce any great strategic insight into new growth opportunities or sources of generic competition. Therefore a second question is usually found in the form of:

2 *What business are we **really** in?*
   This question demands a business definition that is formulated in terms of client needs, i.e. what problems are our clients trying to solve by using our service? It was through this type of questioning that many accountancy firms decided that they were really in the 'business solutions' business rather than the 'auditing and taxation' business. This broad client-need based business definition can, however, be so broad as to be meaningless. Therefore the third question in mission analysis tackles this in the following way:

3 *What business **should** we be in?*
   This question basically addresses the implications of the issues raised in question two. On the basis of the broad client-need based definition of the firm's business this question asks what particular aspects of the business definition give the firm the most insight into ways in which it might grow and towards identifying areas of potential generic competition. However, even this is not enough if mission analysis and resulting mission statements are to be useful in actually running the firm.

4 *What business **can** we be in?*
   This forces the firm to consider its business definition not only in terms of client needs and strategic insight for the future but also in terms of the reality of the firm's existing resources, skills, people, expertise, etc. and the potential ability of the firm to develop the additional resources, people, systems, etc. needed to take advantage of opportunities highlighted, and take a strong competitive position *vis-à-vis* generic competition identified in the mission analysis. This final question imposes the discipline of what the firm

is actually able to do or potentially capable of developing in terms of alternative ways of addressing client needs.

While most organizations in the UK, including an increasing number of professional service firms, have undertaken some form of mission analysis and produced a mission or vision statement as a part of their strategic marketing or corporate planning activities there are a number of dangers that firms need to be aware of if mission analysis is to be useful.

The logic of mission analysis and mission and vision statements with PSFs is that of communication. It is a common experience in seminars, workshops, etc. to ask partners and managers whether or not their firm uses mission analysis and has a formal mission statement. This typically produces one of two responses 'yes – but don't ask me what it is' or 'I'm not sure, but probably.' I have even come across one firm where the managing partner and executive committee had used mission analysis and produced a written mission statement but then decided that this was too commercially sensitive to share with the rest of the partners, let alone the employees! Needless to say a mission statement is unlikely to be of any operational use in terms of actually running the firm and managing its future unless it is communicated to those who are involved in the running of the firm on a day-to-day basis, i.e. everybody in the firm.

In order to be useful in this context of communications it can often be self-defeating to produce mission statements that are three pages long. As a rule of thumb the most useful mission statements, in terms of providing a directional focus for the efforts of all employees, are succinct – only two or three sentences – and are memorable – bullet points, key phrases, alliterations, etc. Most PSFs, however, tend to believe in communication as a one-way process. This can often lead to further problems with mission statements in that if mission analysis is undertaken by the executive committee of a large or even medium-sized PSF the employees at the sharp end of the business, i.e. the service providers, may regard the mission statement produced as unbelievable. If the service provision staff themselves do not believe in the mission statement, regarding it as unrealistic or aspirationally grandiose, then it will simply not be used in running the business. Mission analysis should therefore include participation or at least two-way communication with staff at all levels of the organization.

It is also likely to prove counter-productive to embrace mission analysis as a strategic marketing and planning tool and to proceed to change the firm's mission statement every year. While minor alterations may be necessary, mission statements are most useful and more likely to be remembered and used if they are enduring.

One final facet of mission statement that has been identified by Tom Peters in *Thriving on Chaos*[2] is the ability of mission and vision statements to motivate and 'energize' employees, making explicit the goal that all their work and effort is designed to achieve. If mission statements are to have any 'energizing' benefits for employees then they obviously need to be perceived as not only realistic and achievable but also desirable as far as the employees are concerned.

One practical tip in undertaking mission analysis is to start by putting together a mission analysis of 'what business could we be in?' based upon the benefit derived by the client and to present all the potential missions as a series of concentric circles moving from the 'core' need through increasing levels of abstraction. I recently worked through such a potential mission analysis with a thirty-partner firm of accountants. Each level of the analysis (Figure 6.1) is based upon the need that drives the client to seek the advice and services of an accountancy firm. With each movement away from the 'core' need of fulfilling legal and regulatory requirements, e.g. producing independently audited sets of accounts and filing regular VAT returns, the knowledge, skills, expertise and range of services that need to be offered to satisfy the client-need increase and the parameters of the 'what business are we in' widen. This can be seen to be mirrored in the accountancy profession with many small accountancy firms concentrating only upon the core need of helping clients to fulfil their legal requirements while the largest international accountancy firms see their 'business' in a much wider sense as helping clients to run their

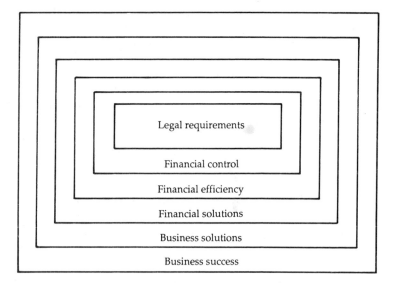

Figure 6.1 *Mission analysis for an accountancy firm*

businesses more successfully and therefore offer almost every conceivable business service from corporate relocation and IT consultancy to executive recruitment and mergers and acquisition advice.

Once a potential mission analysis has been put together the partners may more easily be able to decide which business they are in at the moment and which business they need to be in. This approach can also help partners to see immediately some of the implications for the firm's development of each of the potential mission levels. Many accountants when looking at Figure 6.1 will recognize the client needs but will say we perform at different levels of that analysis in different markets, and in different departments within our firm. If that is the case, and it may well be true in medium and large firms then it is often useful for firms to use market missions or department missions that are separate from those serving other markets or departments. Indeed market missions are actually used by each individual strategic business unit in some of the world's most successful FMCG companies.

Developing marketing objectives and goals

If a mission is seen as the firm's *'raison d'être'* then marketing objectives may be seen as long-range purposes such as growth in fee levels, profitability, etc. and goals as more specific, and usually more highly quantified, targets such as raise fee income from x marketplace by y % in the next 18 months.

In my experience professional service firms don't mind setting relatively woolly longer-term marketing objectives such as 'become market leader in shipping law' or the 'most innovative designers of healthcare facilities', etc. but become very unhappy about setting more specific marketing goals against which it might be possible, even if only qualitatively, to measure the firm's development and progress.

A prescription calling for specific and explicit marketing goals and objectives to be set for a firm, both quantitatively and qualitatively, cascading down into departments, offices or strategic business units, against which the firm can measure its progress may be seen as somewhat old fashioned in strategic marketing terms. Indeed Quinn[3] powerfully illustrates why strategic goals in most commercial organizations remain implicit and ill-defined. However, in most professional service firms the partnership and senior management's ignorance and misconceptions about marketing lead to them being ill-prepared to set specific marketing objectives and goals. Yet without setting goals and demonstrating progress toward objectives marketing is likely to remain a 'black box' or 'black hole' as far as the partners are concerned. In the budgetary in-fighting which also accompanies the beginning of most new financial years in PSFs then being able to demonstrate progress towards explicit goals and objectives is the most powerful form of argument for budget that I have experienced.

The whole strategic goal formulation process may be seen as hierarchical (Figure 6.2). It begins with a mission statement which provides very wide strategic parameters based in terms related to the purpose of the organization. We then progress towards marketing objectives which are elements or variables that the PSF wishes to stress in the longer-term, e.g. auditors to the medical profession, consultants to the oil industry, which are primarily directional and against which progress is measured, usually qualitatively, over a relatively long time-frame. Below objectives in the hierarchy come more specific marketing goals. These are usually short-term, i.e. 6 months or 12 months, and are measurable targets which are considered to be achievable through planned actions within a given time-frame, e.g. we want to attract ten new medical practice clients for audit and financial advice in the Manchester area through running two seminars and writing articles in the medical journals.

Figure 6.2 *Hierarchy in strategic goal formulation*

What goals and objectives should be

Academic empirical investigation of goal setting in the professional service context has been limited. Moutinho[4] in 1988 a study of twenty-eight professional service firms discovered that most firms' primary goals are set in terms of sales volume (fee income) and profitability. Following these criteria in order of use were firm image goals, return on investment, and market share. These results mirror my own practical experiences in PSFs where partnerships are willing to set broad targets for fee income and to a lesser extent partnership profitability but are less than happy to set associated marketing goals in terms of image, positioning and, especially, market share. The reluctance to use market share in goal setting is particularly noteworthy given the level of debate concerning the nature of the relationship between market share and profitability that has dominated the world of strategic marketing in the recent past.[5]

Irrespective of the actual criteria upon which goals and objectives are set in professional service firm's, marketing academics have proposed some prescriptive advice for practitioners. Kotler's[6] textbook prescription is typical of these. Kotler's prescription is that objectives and goals should be:

Hierarchical: firms pursue multiple goals and objectives in most cases and therefore in order to provide focused effort in planning and implementation the firm's goals should be explicit and prioritized.

Quantitative: most writers induce practitioners to set quantified, measurable goals whenever possible. I would add a note of caution to this in that this can lead to a tendency to focus only upon those things which can be easily measured. Remember that just because you can't measure something it doesn't mean that it's not important!

Realistic: setting realistic target levels for goals is also seen to be important. Unrealistic targets can and do demotivate staff and lead to less effort towards achievement than if no target has been set at all. This can be particularly damaging if evaluation and reward are linked to targets.

Consistent: there has to be a recognition that there are trade-offs to be made between mutually exclusive objectives and goals such as short-term profit vs long-term growth, growth vs stability, etc.

A further note of caution should finally be recognized in terms of strategic and marketing goals and objectives. While prescriptions calling for hierarchies of objectives, and my own advice to actually set some quantifiable marketing goals, are valid I recently experienced a preliminary planning workshop in the regional office of a large national service organization in which executives, unused to planning, were presented with a list of ten 'key' objectives. Each of the objectives was described as 'vital to the survival and prosperity of this organization'. Many of these were actually mutually exclusive or at least conflicting and left the planning group in reality 'aimless'. These objectives should have been prioritized at least and preferably worked on individually by planning teams in a 'chunking' approach. Do not set many objectives, it will simply confuse your people and dissipate their efforts.

Situation analysis

The strategic marketing audit stage of the marketing planning process is essentially concerned with the simple question of 'where are we now?' in terms of both strategic and marketing resources, capabilities, strengths and weaknesses, with emphasis upon how we as a firm measure up to client and market expectations and perceptions, and how we stand *vis-à-vis* competition. In many PSFs this stage of the planning process is often perceived as having been implicitly carried out and known by the partners and senior managers of the firm as a part of managing the business on a day to day basis. Only rarely, however, is a firm sufficiently advanced and systematic in its management practices to be able to claim in reality that they have little to gain from a formal strategic audit of both the entire firm and its marketing.

Approaches to the strategic marketing audit usually adopt the form of categories of internal issues to be examined, or checklists of questions to be answered in terms of strengths and weaknesses. In one of the surprisingly few academic analyses of this stage of the marketing

Table 6.1 *Categories for assessing strengths and weaknesses*

Category	Attributes
Organization	Organization structure
	Management and decision making
	Standard operating procedures
	Planning and control systems
Personnel	Employee attitude
	Technical skills
	Experience
	Management skills
	Training
Marketing	Partners' marketing involvement
	Knowledge of client needs
	Breadth and depth of service offerings
	Service quality
	Image and perceived position
	Market segmentation
	Professional reputation
Technical	Technical expertise resource
	Technical training/updates
	Technical research
	Information on technical developments
Finance	Financial size
	Service profitability
	Segment profitability
	Growth pattern

Adapted by the author from Stevenson, H. H. (1976), 'Defining Corporate Strengths and Weaknesses', *Sloan Management Review*, Spring.

planning process Stevenson[7] suggested the broad categories of situation analysis shown in Table 6.1.

Other more specific checklists are available in the marketing literature, although outside the professional service context.[8] At the end of this section of the book is an appendix of the issues and key questions that I have found useful in marketing strategic marketing audits in professional service firms.

In discussing situation analysis and the strategic marketing audit professionals seem keen to talk about, discuss and learn tools and techniques of planning. A particular favourite in terms of situational analysis is the ubiquitous SWOT (strengths, weaknesses, opportunities, threats) analysis.

SWOT analysis is a simple approach to situation analysis providing a framework in which partners and managers can order their thinking about their internal capabilities and shortcomings (strengths and weaknesses) and their view of the marketplace and competitive environment (opportunities and threats) and, by the positioning of the internal and external analysis of the current situation facing the firm, focus the mind on how the firm can best interact with its environment.

The simplicity of the SWOT approach (Figure 6.3) has elevated it to the status of being the most widely used management tool in strategic and marketing planning. Stevenson[7] and others have, however, demonstrated that SWOT analysis is also a much abused management tool open to bias, subjectivity, unwarranted optimism and the use of historical criteria in evaluating strengths but normative criteria in the evaluation of weaknesses. All of these implicit operational problems in using SWOT usually lead to the output of the analysis being bland, universal looking, full of 'motherhood' and lacking in strategic marketing insight.

In attempting to capitalize upon SWOT's essential simplicity and its 'user-friendly' status Piercy and Giles[9] have developed a more

Strengths	Weaknesses
Opportunities	Threats

Figure 6.3 *The conventional SWOT framework*

rigorous form of SWOT analysis which I have found to be extremely useful in undertaking strategic marketing planning in professional service firms. This approach takes the traditional SWOT framework and applies five new 'groundrules' which ensure that the output of the analysis both gives better strategic insight and focuses upon the critical interface between the firm and its clients. These new SWOT rules are:

1 *Focus*

    Traditionally SWOT analyses, particularly in the professional service context have been undertaken upon the firm as a whole. This level of analysis is insufficient for productive use of the model. SWOT analyses therefore need to be undertaken upon more specific areas such as a specific service-market, a specific client segment, a specific competitor, fee schedules in a particular market, etc. Trying to use SWOT at a 'global' level usually produces meaningless results. If a global view is needed then we can simply undertake SWOT on each of the critical areas that make up the 'global' view.

2 *Shared vision*

    The SWOT framework lends itself to being used by planning teams. In being used in this team setting the model benefits from the different types of information brought to the team by individual members. In firms with no marketing information system the types and levels of information that SWOT analysis elicits from team members can be quite astounding and in most cases it is the first time that this information has been explicitly shared within the firm. SWOT analysis can therefore provide a mechanism for bringing together information and allowing the team to negotiate a consensus on how they, and thus the firm, see both themselves (i.e. the firm, department, etc.) and their relationship with the outside world.

3 *Client orientation*

    This is a particularly painful and worthwhile discipline to introduce into SWOT analysis. This applies to the strengths and weaknesses section of the analysis. Nothing can be entered into either the strengths or weaknesses section unless (a) clients would *recognize* the point, (b) clients would *agree* with the analysis and (c) clients would *value* the point made. This is one of the simplest ways of helping partners and managers to identify attributes of the firm that are particular strengths or weaknesses.

    This approach has particular merit in that it forces those involved in the planning team to think in client-centred terms and focus upon client needs throughout the process. It also has some merit in that you can actually test the SWOT against client views if you wish (although the threat of doing this is often sufficient to induce partners, etc. to adopt a client-centred view!). This approach also overcomes the familiar assertion from partners, etc. that 'our greatest strength is also our greatest weakness'. Nothing in this model can be a strength *and* a weakness – this merely means that the issue has not been broken down sufficiently into the specific aspects that, from the client's point of view, represent strengths and weaknesses, (see Table 6.2).

Table 6.2 *Client-centred view of strengths and weaknesses*

'Old' strength and weakness	New client-centred view	
	Strength	Weakness
'A large firm'	Wide service range	Bureaucratic
	Depth of technical expertise	Limited partner access
	High status reassures clients	Discontinuity of personal contact
'An old established firm'	Trustworthy	Old fashioned
	Experienced	Lacking in innovation
	Stable producers	Inflexible

Occasionally a planning team will insist that some attribute of the firm, even though it doesn't pass the client orientation test, is too important to leave out of the analysis. In such cases this 'hidden' strength may be included but only if the group will consider what might appropriately be done to communicate these 'hidden strengths' to clients in a way that would add value to their services.

4 *Environmental analysis*

There is always a temptation, in undertaking SWOT analysis, to be subjective about the environment (i.e. the opportunities and threats) part of the matrix. This is often the result of the lack of relevant client, market and competitor information that is typically available within professional service firms. SWOT can be useful in demonstrating to partners and managers just how little they know about the environment, and critical information gaps can be identified for marketing research, etc.

In order to enforce objectivity, those using SWOT can only enter in the opportunities and threats quadrants environmental facts and issues which are completely external to the firm, i.e. they would exist whether the firm existed or not. This also prevents planners jumping the gun and putting their tactical and action ideas in the opportunities quadrants. It is vital for the final part of SWOT that planners do not confuse their own action ideas (strategies) with what is actually in existence in the environment.

5 *Structured strategy generation*

When the cells of the SWOT matrix have been completed following the Piercy and Giles 'groundrules' then the SWOT can actually be used as a mechanism for generating two kinds of structured strategies:

(a) *Matching strategies*: the focus here is upon ways of matching the strengths identified within the firm with the opportunities that exist in the marketplace. Strengths which do not map onto opportunities have little real value in the specific area while opportunities for which no internal strength is apparent may give ideas as to resources, competencies, etc. that may need to be developed internally. Planners should not forget to check out the possibilities of weaknesses within the firm mapping onto threats in the environment – this could be a predictor of serious problems ahead.

(b) *Conversion strategies*: here the focus is upon the internal weaknesses and external threats that have been identified in the matrix, with the aim of generating strategies that will either neutralize these issues or, conceivably and ideally, convert weaknesses into strengths and threats into opportunities.

Using SWOT analysis with such a client-centred approach can prove to be an excellent mechanism for undertaking basic situation analysis in strategic marketing planning. It provides a basis for teamwork in planning and is useful for both negotiating consensus views within the firm and identifying information gaps, needs and requirements. It can also be a tool for generating some strategy options to be considered in the planning process.

Another approach familiar to many partners and managers in the situation analysis stage of the planning process is the product portfolio matrix developed by the Boston Consulting Group.[10] This matrix is an original attempt to get firms to take a balanced portfolio approach to the range of services they offer in order to ensure long-term growth and development and sound internal investment decisions concerning individual services and groups of services.

The underlying logic of the Boston model depends upon two important strategic marketing concepts: the product life cycle and experience curves.

The product life cycle

Most managers and directors of manufacturing companies would agree that products seem to go through some sort of life cycle over time. This may also be true of service 'products'. The product life cycle is typically shown as an 's' shaped curve as in Figure 6.4.

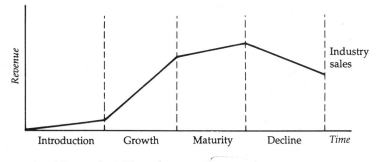

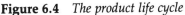

Figure 6.4 *The product life cycle*

A product or service is therefore envisaged as often moving through several distinct phases over time. At introduction initial market acceptance is limited and thus growth is slow. At this stage the product or service will be generating few returns due to marketing and other expenses involved in introducing a new product or service to a market. During the growth phase those products or services that manage to survive the introductory stage may then enjoy a period of faster growth as increasing market acceptance and awareness is achieved and the firm may begin to enjoy some returns on its investment in terms of profit. As the product enters its mature stage growth *slows* and competition for market share increases. Overall profitability declines and often product proliferation occurs and margins are squeezed in the face of competitor strategies. Finally, there is a decline period in which the market growth rate goes into reverse and competitors often begin to drop out of the marketplace as profitability and margins decline.

While many readers may recognize the common-sense validity of the life cycle concept there are a number of problems with using it as an operational planning tool in the professional service context:

1 *What life cycle?* The classic 's' curve life cycle seems to work, and is in fact based upon aggregate demand for products such as stainless steel, electricity, etc. Life cycle curves for individual products from individual manufacturers will look nothing like the composite average industry curve. Life cycles will vary enormously in shape and time dependent upon whether you are looking at individual service from one firm, all the generic offerings of that type from one firm, or all the services offered to the marketplace of that type by all suppliers.

2 *Where are we on the life cycle?* Actually positioning one of your services on a life cycle is in practical terms impossible to do with any degree of accuracy. If you cannot be sure where you are on the life cycle curve then it is of very limited use in planning marketing

99

strategies, etc. Even if a firm, through analysis of historical service and industry data, current position and competitive analysis, believes that the characteristics of a service point to a particular stage of the 'classic' life cycle then there is still the problem of knowing just how long that phase is likely to last, e.g. Heinz beans and Cadburys Dairy Milk brands are over one hundred years old and have probably been in the 'mature' phase for most of their 'lives'.

3 *Many professional service life cycles are regulatory* Depending upon how a firm wishes to define a service there is an argument that in many professional service sectors the life cycle of an individual service is dictated more through legislation and regulatory change than simple demand, supply and the diffusion of innovation. This is particularly true in the legal and accountancy professions, and to a lesser degree in consulting engineering, architecture, etc. In other professions the critical component of life cycle effect may be technology and research developments, e.g. medicine, dentistry, veterinary services, etc.

4 *Empirical validity of life cycle concept* In spite of the 'common-sense' logic of the life cycle concept the empirical research to test its validity is still relatively scarce (Doyle, 1976).[11] Further, the empirical evidence that does exist is almost exclusively based in the manufacturing sector. Thus while in the world of manufacturing and consumer goods the life cycle concept may have some validity, even here it is really too imprecise to use as an operational tool for making planning decisions. This is even more true in the service sector where the concept has less empirical validity and potentially even more difficulty in operational use.

The second strategic concept underlying the Boston Consulting Group approach is that of experience effects. Based upon a series of studies by the BCG and PIMS, building upon the earlier work on learning curves, the experience effect holds that with increases in cumulative volume of production the unit costs of production will fall. The empirical support for the experience effect or experience 'curve' as it has become widely known is persuasive. The sources of the decreases in unit costs associated with accumulated volume of production have been identified in three basic areas by Day and Montgomery:[12]

1 *Learning* Encompassing all the elements of human input into production including increasing skills and changing the way work is organized to produce. This can also hold for marketing activities such as new product development.

2   *Technological improvement*   New production processes, product standardization and automation of human inputs can also yield substantial experience effects, particularly in capital intensive industries.
3   *Economies of scale*   Savings from increased efficiency due to size are another source of the experience effect.

One of the most significant strategic implications of the experience curve effect is in the relationship between profitability and market share. Simple economics suggests that if the experience curve effect holds true then it affords the potential for the firm with the greatest market share (and thus most rapidly accumulating volume) to enjoy the lowest costs per unit and therefore to be the most profitable supplier in the industry. This relationship between profitability and market share has subsequently been illustrated in the PIMS studies in the USA (Buzzell and Gale).[13]

Again the basis for the experience curve concept has grown out of studies in the manufacturing sector, although one of the foundation studies reported by Headley[14] gave an experience 'slope' for a US supplier of life insurance policies. However, in spite of the lack of empirical validations of experience curve effects in the service sector, the logic may well apply in the professional service sector, particularly in the area of learning effects on the part of professional and administrative staff, and technological development and the 'industrialization' of service, e.g. computer audits, computer-aided design in engineering and architecture, computer-based diagnosis in medicine, etc.

The Boston Consulting Group combined the concepts of product life cycle and experience curves in a portfolio planning model that has been widely used by strategic and marketing planners and consultants and appears in many organizations' planning manuals. The product portfolio matrix is used in multi-business or multi-product/service firms in order to aid investment decisions within the business and in order to attempt to ensure stable earnings and growth in the future.

Such a portfolio approach forces planners to examine each service or strategic business unit (SBU) both in the context of its own environment and in its contribution to the overall goals of the firm. The classic BCG product portfolio matrix is shown in Figure 6.5. In the BCG approach relative market share, based upon experience effects and the PIMS results, is a proxy for profitability. The 'relative' part of this proxy measurement is relative to the market share enjoyed by the market leader. The second dimension of the matrix is market growth rate which is a proxy for product life cycle which can help predict the cash requirement of the various SBUs or products/services. Individual

101

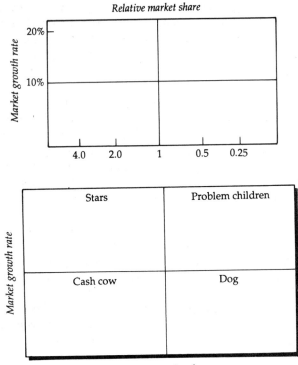

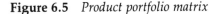

Figure 6.5 *Product portfolio matrix*

products/services or SBUs are usually located on the matrix and represented by a circle, the size of which represents the revenue generation of the product/service or SBU.

Having located each of your firm's products/services on the growth share matrix the model can provide some guidelines as to the desired movement of the product/service within the matrix and thus the 'appropriate' strategies and desired internal investment and cash movement within the firm.

Cash cows – products/services falling in this quadrant have high market share in slow growing markets. They are profitable and should be generating considerable cash as they are unlikely to need massive investment due to the slow growth in the marketplace. The obvious strategy with cash cows is to protect market share and ensure that you take at least the same share of the new business that comes along.

102

Stars – these products/services are also likely to be profitable services since they have a high market share. However, the rapidly growing market may well mean stars are net cash absorbers as significant investment is likely to be involved in taking a large share of the new business in a rapidly growing market. Stars are important as they will provide the cash cows of the future for the firm when the market growth rate has slowed.

Problem children – these have relatively small market shares in rapidly growing markets. They are unlikely to be profitable and are usually absorbers of cash. The options here are fairly clear: either the firm invests heavily in order to gain a disproportionately high share of the new business, e.g. by buying/merging with a competitor product/ service or the business is divested or withdrawn.

Dogs – these have low market share in 'mature' markets in which it is often prohibitively expensive to gain market share in any sensible way. These businesses are often net cash absorbers although they may produce small positive cash flows in some cases. The main strategic options here are to redefine the market through segmentation and attempt to dominate a niche or harvest the business by taking whatever cash it produces but investing little back in the business. Finally the business may be divested or the service withdrawn.

A note of caution

Professionals, when exposed to the BCG approach, are apt to see the growth share matrix as the solution to their strategic and marketing planning problems. The matrix can be a useful tool in providing some insight into potential strategy options in professional service firms, particularly the medium and large multi-service firms. However, it is a tool that is easily abused and needs to be used with caution for a number of reasons:

Underlying assumptions – the assumptions underlying the BCG approach and their applicability in the particular context of the professional service firm's business need to be validated before the matrix can be used. If there is no obvious life cycle in the service market being analysed or market share is not a good indicator of profitability in the specific context of the firm, then the matrix is invalidated and cannot be used.

Measurement – there are obvious problems in agreeing the

measurements that are appropriate for the scaling in terms of what, exactly, constitutes high and low market share and what represents high or low market growth rate.

Market definition – the model is open to manipulation through the definition of the market served by each service product, e.g. are we talking about the market for engineering bridge work services or are we talking about the market for bridge reinforcement services in the north east of England? The definition and redefinition of markets can (and does) completely change where service offerings will be placed in the matrix.

Decision making – the product portfolio matrix *cannot* make strategic choices for a firm. At best it can provide insight into potential options. In too many firms the model becomes a decision *making* tool rather than a decision *support* tool.

References

1   Levitt, T. (1960), 'Marketing myopia', *Harvard Business Review*, July/ August, pp. 45–56.
2   Peters, T. (1989), *Thriving on Chaos*, London: Pan.
3   Quinn, J. B. (1975), 'Strategic goals: process and politics', *Sloan Management Review*, Fall, pp. 34–46.
4   Moutinho, L. (1989), 'Goal setting process and typologies: the case of professional services', *Journal of Professional Services Marketing*, vol. 4, no. 2, pp. 83–100.
5   Buzzell, R. D. and Gale, R. T. (1987), *The Pims principles – linking strategy to performance*, New York: The Free Press; Jacobson, R. and Aaker, D. A. (1985), 'Is market share all that it's cracked up to be?', *Journal of Marketing*, vol. 49, no. 4, pp. 11–22.
6   Kotler, P. (1984), *Marketing Management: Analysis, Planning and Control* (5th edn), Englewood Cliffs: Prentice-Hall, pp. 49–50.
7   Stevenson, H. H. (1976), 'Defining corporate strengths and weaknesses', *Sloan Management Review*, Spring.
8   Kotler, P. (1977), 'From sales obsession to marketing effectiveness', *Harvard Business Review*, Nov–Dec, p. 68; Kotler, P., Gregor, W. and Rogers, W. (1977), 'The marketing audit comes of age', *Sloan Management Review*, Winter, pp. 25–44; Wilson, A. (1982), *Aubrey Wilson's Marketing Checklists*, London: McGraw-Hill.
9   Piercy, N. and Giles, W. (1990), 'Revitalising and operationalising the SWOT model in strategic planning, *University of Wales Business and Economic Review*, no. 3, pp. 3–10.
10 Boston Consulting Group (1970), 'The product portfolio', *Perspectives*, no. 66, Boston: The Boston Consulting Group.
11 Doyle, P. (1976), 'The Realities of the product life cycle', *Quarterly Review of Marketing*, Summer, pp. 1–6.

12 Day, G. S. and Montgomery, D. B. (1983), 'Diagnosing the experience curve', *Journal of Marketing*, vol. **47**, Spring, pp. 44–58.
13 Buzzell, R. D. and Gale, R. T. op. cit.
14 Headley, B. (1976), 'A fundamental approach to strategy development', *Long Range Planning*, December, pp. 2–11.

7 Environmental analysis

One of the most important decisions that has to be addressed in any comprehensive strategic marketing plan is the market coverage decision. However, few professional service firms ever make an explicit choice of which target markets they wish to serve and those which they are going to ignore. This process of market segmentation and target market selection is perhaps the most critical part of strategic marketing planning and is therefore worth examining in some detail.

The market coverage decision is, in essence, a simple choice between three basic options: undifferentiated marketing, concentrated marketing and differentiated marketing.

Undifferentiated marketing is the service equivalent of 'mass marketing' in the FMCG sector. This approach entails the firm appealing to the entire potential marketplace with one marketing mix programme (Figure 7.1).

Figure 7.1 *Undifferentiated marketing*

This approach is characteristic of 'general practice' professional service firms who attempt to supply whatever type of their professional service is needed by any clients in the aggregate marketplace. This undifferentiated approach is often adopted by small, one and two partner professional service firms, and also by some of the largest national and international firms within the various professions. This type of approach has obvious disadvantages in the difficulties in meeting the differing service needs of clients and usually leads to a lack of perceived differentiation in the marketplace.

Concentrated marketing is the antithesis of the undifferentiated approach. Here the firm has analysed the aggregate potential market and identified a single client segment that it is best capable of effectively servicing and that will enable the firm to achieve its desired objectives. This concentrated approach (Figure 7.2) is often labelled 'niche' marketing in the management press (and even 'crineau' by the consultants!).

Figure 7.2 *Concentrated marketing*

The aim of the concentrated marketing approach is obviously to establish a competitive differentiation and comparative advantage by developing a specialized service offering tailored to the needs of the specific target segment. I have recently come across two good examples of this, one a small three-partner law firm in Leeds who deal almost exclusively with providing legal services to the package holiday industry, and the other a small consultancy engineering firm that specializes in providing project risk appraisals to international banks funding overseas development projects.

The concentrated approach while being more 'market-oriented' than the undifferentiated option, and often allowing higher margins, is also the most inherently risky market coverage decision. The firm is then effectively tied to the fortunes of the target client segment and opportunities for diversified growth are likely to be limited.

The final market coverage option is labelled 'differentiated marketing' which is essentially a hybrid option (Figure 7.3). Differentiated marketing entails segmenting the aggregate potential market and choosing a number of different client/service target segments upon which to concentrate developing service offerings and marketing mixes designed to appeal to the specific needs of the segments.

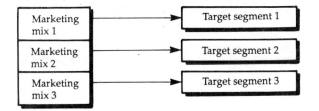

Figure 7.3 *Differentiated marketing*

This multiple segment approach is particularly useful in relatively fragmented marketplaces. It does allow the firm to differentiate itself from other professional service suppliers and is also less inherently risky than the concentrated approach. However, the costs of developing service offerings and marketing mix programmes specifically catering for the different needs of the target client segments can be high.

Market segmentation is critical to the strategic marketing planning process and has been described as 'one of the most fundamental and dominant concepts of modern marketing'.[1] In essence, however, market segmentation is a relatively simple concept describing the division of a total market into two or more groups of buyers where each identified group is internally homogeneous in some way but is externally different from the other identified groups.

In most cases the market coverage options of concentrated and differentiated marketing are likely to be the most effective for professional service firms. There are two obvious and major reasons for this. First, in almost any profession you can think of there is a high degree of 'customization' of the service offering needed because each individual client is likely to have slightly different requirements, and the diversity of client needs across the whole of the potential market for a particular professional service is likely to be enormous. Therefore, attempting to service all potential clients with their widely differing needs is likely to be practically impossible for most professional service firms. Second, the nature of professional services makes it difficult for PSFs to achieve a competitive differentiation in the marketplace. Achieving differentiation is likely to be much easier if a segment-based market coverage approach is chosen. In spite of these advantages, however, most professional service firms seem to be largely unable to focus effectively upon either one or a few client segments, and a general practice approach develops even in sophisticated PSFs who will often claim to have segmented the entire potential market and be attacking the whole aggregate market as separate segments. Many PSFs see the value and strategic merit of adopting a segment-based approach to their marketplace but are then incapable of turning away enquiries from potential clients outside the agreed target markets. It is almost impossible to get to a stage where partners and staff of a PSF can respond to an enquiry with 'I'm afraid this firm doesn't provide that type of service, can I suggest that you contact XYZ and Co, who do' more likely is 'I'm sure we can help you in some way, can I check with my colleagues and get back to you with a proposal'. Most firms are incapable of turning down even small work that doesn't fit in with the firm's focus and development strategies. This can cause enormous problems to those trying to establish a competitive differentiation in the marketplace.

At present most professional service firms demonstrate the market segmentation approach that they adopt in their organizational structure. By far the most common approach is to base segmentation upon the services which target client segments purchase, e.g. accountancy firms are commonly structured with audit departments, tax departments, insolvency departments, etc. Law firms commonly have service-based departments such as corporate, litigation, property, shipping, pensions, etc. Medical services are usually offered on the same basis of organization and segmentation according to the service specialization or type being provided. A smaller minority of professional service firms organize and segment their markets on the basis of simple client characteristics, e.g. industry groups, etc. Few professional service firms step outside this 'normal' approach to market segmentation.

There are, however, an almost infinite number of ways in which PSFs could possibly segment their marketplaces and it may be that taking a new segmentation approach, one that is different from that of your competitors, is one of the best levers for building both competitive differentiation and comparative advantage in the medium term.

Bases for segmenting markets

There are numerous potential bases for segmentation that may be utilized either singly or in conjunction with others in order to segment the market for PSFs. These categories of bases include:

Geographic regions, particular cities, urban, suburban, rural etc.
Demographic (organizational) ownership structure, size, industry, age, etc.
Demographic (consumer) family life cycle, age, sex, occupation, education, etc.
Behavioural usage rate, decision process stage, referral source, buying structure, etc.
Benefits most important service attribute, type of problem, basic needs, etc.

Potentially the most fruitful basis for segmenting a market is on the basis of the benefits sought by the client and writers have suggested that so-called 'benefit segmentation'[2] should be the preferred base in business to business markets.[3] The process of 'benefit segmentation' usually involves the grouping of existing and potential clients on the basis of the similarity of the buying criteria that they use in selecting a professional service adviser. This can provide a good surrogate for the benefits sought by clients through using a professional service and can give insight into factors which drive the purchase decisions of clients.[4] A market segmentation based upon benefits sought by clients is particularly useful in identifying market opportunities in terms of current client needs and dissatisfied segments.

The process of market segmentation, in the light of its strategic importance, is worth some consideration. The 'classical' approach to market segmentation prescribes a simple six stage approach to the whole segmentation process:[5]

1 Determine the needs and characteristics of clients and potential clients for the services that the firm offers.
2 Analyse client needs and characteristics for differences and similarities and form segments around these.
3 Develop a profile of the client segments identified.
4 Select the client segment(s) which the firm is best able to service and that will enable the firm to achieve its objectives.
5 Position the firm's service in these target segments in relation to competition service offerings.
6 Establish an appropriate marketing plan for each client segment.

While this approach looks relatively simple it does in fact cause enormous problems for professional service firms and usually results in no serious market segmentation being undertaken at all for a number of reasons.

1 Any segmentation exercise involves the collection of, and access to, at least some rudimentary marketing research. In the majority of firms even this rudimentary data is unavailable.
2 Even where such data exists significant data analysis is often needed to uncover similarities and differences and provide bases for clustering clients into groups.
3 When segments can be identified marketers and professionals are often inclined to attempt to service all the segments possible rather than concentrating upon a smaller number.

These are significant and real problems in operationalizing market segmentation. However, they are not insoluble. Realistically, segmentation cannot be undertaken without some basic marketing information. This does not mean that if you have not got a £30,000 research budget then market segmentation is impossible. In-house client and market surveys and client focus groups, if handled objectively by those with some knowledge of research techniques and practices, can yield enough information to segment a market. This is possible because segmentation is not, as many professionals and marketers seem to believe, primarily a matter of data analysis. There is a widespread fallacy amongst marketers that if only they could collect sufficient client information and analyse the data in sufficient depth then market segments would automatically drop out which would enable the firm to wipe out its competitors. Such a view is obviously fallacious for every marketer always seems to require more and better information when perfect information is obviously impossible. Even if it were possible and we could somehow cram it into a computer, each competitor with the same information would end up with the same segmentation analysis and firms would experience no comparative and competitive advantage.

The harsh truth, which has to be faced in PSFs by both professionals and marketers, is that segmentation has to be undertaken with limited, imperfect, client and market information, and that the analysis of the information and formation of segments is more about creative thinking and strategic insight than data analysis and statistical techniques.

In the context of benefit segmentation one approach that I have found useful in planning with professional service firms is an extension of the client–service matrix described in Chapter 3. This is a simple process which involves mapping out the services provided by the firm in a given area of business and the client groups or segments currently used by the firm in a matrix form, e.g. for an accountancy firm of twenty partners in their owner-managed business department the client–service matrix may look like Figure 7.4.

					Services				
Clients	Audit	Financial review	Book-keeping	VAT advice	VAT returns	TAX returns	Tax planning	Payroll	Business planning
Farmers			●			●	●		
Retailers		●			●		●	●	
Manufacturers	●						●		
Medical		●	●				●		
Legal		●							
Services								●	●

Figure 7.4 *Client–service matrix for owner-managed business department*

This simple matrix lists the major service offerings of the firm, the major client groups served and the primary services utilized by each of the client groups. In terms of using this matrix as a starting point for a market segmentation exercise then the approach is twofold.

First, the obvious question – are we as a firm specialist in servicing a particular type of client? In this example the firm obviously provides the greatest number of services to retail clients. However, there are a number of service offerings that are not used by this client group and, considering the current service range, the firm is obviously clearly not a specialist in providing accounting and business services to retailers. This is not to say that it would be impossible to develop a strategy focusing upon the specific service needs of retailers but at the moment this does not constitute an effective segment-based approach.

Second, the firm can examine the other side of the matrix and begin to consider a generic service-offering-based segmentation strategy. In terms of service segments the firm's most popular services are tax planning and financial review. Adopting a market-oriented approach to service segmentation the firm can work backwards to consider the client needs and benefits derived from each of these services. In this case tax planning may be seen as a 'financial efficiency' benefit segment and financial review as a 'financial control/security' benefit segment. It may then be possible to work forward from these two benefit segments to consider different service offerings and allied marketing mixes for each.

In many cases a multiple segmentation base approach is appropriate and allows more room for developing new ways of looking at client markets, focusing service and marketing development efforts, and increasing the potential and competitive differentiation possible in a development strategy. In the above case the firm may well consider a segment-based approach built around financial efficiency services for small and medium-sized businesses, and financial control/security services for service businesses and professional practices. This may provide a niche strategy that can move the firm away from its present 'general practice' approach and lever its ability to achieve competitive differentiation and gain some comparative advantage in the medium term.

Having considered market segmentation as a basic approach to developing marketing strategies and plans there is also the question of exactly what makes a segmentation analysis useful to a firm and how a firm should choose which segments to attack.

The preceding section on market segmentation shows quite clearly that there is no 'right' way to segment a market. There are a huge number of bases for segmentation and many possibilities for multiple bases. However, while any market can be segmented in almost an infinite number of ways, not all of these, and indeed most of them, are unlikely to be useful. In order to be useful to a firm the segments identified by a segmentation analysis should have the following characteristics:[6]

Measurability this concerns the firm's ability to estimate or forecast the likely number of existing and potential clients in the segment and thus enable a probable market value to be assessed. This may be difficult in many segments but is important in terms of the decision about which segments to concentrate upon.

Accessibility this characteristic concerns the ability of the firm to effectively reach and service this client segment. Considerations here will include displacement of existing service providers, cost of developing specific services and ability to effectively communicate services, benefits, differentiation, etc., to the segment.

Substantiality this relates to the sizes of the segments identified in terms of total spend, potential market share, likely fee income, profit margins, etc. In most cases firms will opt to concentrate upon the largest possible segment that they can effectively reach and service.

Actionability at the end of the day a segment is worthless even if it is large, potentially profitable and easily reached via communications, if the firm lacks the ability or will to develop its resources sufficiently to be able to develop specialized, specific service offerings and marketing programmes targeted at the segment.

These characteristics of effective segmentation can be used as one way of determining both the potential usefulness of the segmentation analysis and as a base for deciding upon which, and how many, segments the firm should attempt to service. There are obviously a number of other internal and external factors which are likely to affect the decision of which segments to serve, and one useful way of determining these, and thus of choosing between segments, is the 'business position assessment' outlined in the following chapter.

The environmental analysis, i.e. the 'external' part of the situation audit stage of a strategic marketing planning process focuses not only upon the marketplace in terms of clients and segmentation but also upon competitors. While most professionals recognize the importance of the competitive environment in determining their own development strategies and plans, few firms actively monitor, in any systematic and regular way, the activities and strategies of competitors. There are two main reasons why this is the case. First, most partners and managers while picking up information about competitors' activities as part of their normal professional working life lack a coherent framework in which to bring together all the disparate information about competitors that exists. Second, if a framework for analysing competitor activity is provided firms are often incapable of finding enough information to make judgements about competition and levels of competition in target markets.

While the reasons for most PSFs' lack of competitive analysis on a formal and systematic basis as an ongoing part of the strategic marketing planning process are identifiable, few firms have done anything to solve the problem. However, progress can and should be made on both issues.

In terms of frameworks for analysing competition the academic world has, for once, produced some models of competition which can be useful in the real world in addressing the vital questions of 'who are our competitors' and 'what creates competition in our marketplace'. The most important work is that of Michael Porter[7] of the Harvard Business School whose work has influenced strategy development in both the academic and 'real' world. Porter's model of competition and the factors influencing the degree of competition have some validity in the concept of markets for professional services.

In the Porter model (Figure 7.5) there are five basic sources of influence upon the degree of rivalry, i.e. the level of competition in a marketplace. The weight of each of these will depend upon the type of service or product market analysed.

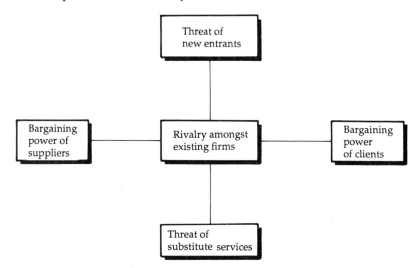

Figure 7.5 *Porter's model of competition*

At the centre of Porter's model are the competitive strategies and tactics of those PSFs already competing to service the clients in the marketplace. Porter suggests that competition is likely to be greatest in marketplaces in which suppliers are roughly equal in terms of size and power, market growth rate is slow, the service lacks differentiation and/or there are costs associated with switching to alternative suppliers, exit barriers are high and rivals are diverse in 'strategies, origins and personality'.

The threat of new entrants is nearly always a factor that needs consideration in analysing the likely competition in a marketplace.

This is particularly true in the professional service context since in many service markets the 'start up' costs of entry are relatively low and small PSFs are formed, merge and disband all the time. A relatively new consideration for many service markets is now also to be found in the threat of new competition outside the UK, or outside the 'traditional' geographic service market boundary, e.g. many of the largest non-London based law firms are to be found in Leeds serving northern corporate clients. However, the development in communications between the north and London in terms of road, rail and air links as well as technical communications advances in terms of facsimile, teleconferencing, etc., have led to the increasing presence of 'City' law firms in markets traditionally served by Leeds firms.

Threat of substitute services is becoming an increasingly important determinant of future competition in PSF marketplaces, particularly in the light of the service development activities amongst the larger firms in each profession. Threats of substitute services have traditionally come from rival firms within a profession. Since professional service offerings are in essence solutions to client problems, different firms within a profession may offer different service solutions, e.g. does a small client of an accountancy firm require an audit or merely a financial review; both are potential service solutions to a similar client problem. However, a feature of the recent development of professional service marketplaces is the increasing threat of substitute services from other types of professional service firm, e.g. tax planning is now primarily seen by clients as an accountancy rather than a legal service, accountancy firms now dominate many management consultancy marketplaces, design–build firms are challenging architects and consulting engineers, banks and building societies are set to challenge solicitors for conveyancing services, etc.

It is vital that, with the trend towards substitute services, firms, when analysing marketplaces and likely competition, define the markets in terms of client needs and not their own professional service offering. It is no longer sufficient to analyse existing direct competitors and formulate competitive strategies. PSFs now also need to analyse potential indirect competitors, i.e. other possible service solutions for the client's basic problem and needs, and build this analysis into the firm's competitive strategies.

The remaining forces affecting existing and potential competition in a service marketplace are the bargaining power of suppliers and clients. In any professional service context the suppliers are the sources of professionals and professionals themselves in the labour market. The production of fewer graduates, especially those following vocational degrees, and the resulting competition amongst PSFs for graduate recruits pushes up the costs of recruitment which has knock-on effects for the costs of part- and post-qualified professionals, and will tend to lower margins and overall profitability of firms. Perhaps more important in the recent past has been the increasing power of clients.

The traditional marketplace relationship between PSF suppliers and clients whereby clients were grateful that a professional deigned to give them advice and service solutions has changed dramatically over the last twenty years. Client expectations are now growing, service quality is replacing cost as a key part of client selection and evaluation procedures, and in many professional service marketplaces power in the professional–client relationship has shifted significantly towards the client. This is particularly true in markets in which clients are relatively concentrated, the professional services are largely undifferentiated and in markets in which clients are experiencing recession in the private sector, or declining funding in the public sector. This has been experienced on the client side by increasing the number of projects, assignments, etc. that are put out to 'tender' and the introduction of 'beauty parades', (competitive presentations), and increasing demand for fuller proposals, and on the supplier side through 'development pricing', 'low-balling', etc.

The Porter model, while appearing initially simplistic and disingenuous, can and does provide a general framework with which to structure the firm's thinking and analysis of existing and potential competition within a service marketplace.

Simple frameworks for competitor analysis can also be built around simple worksheets or spreadsheets within PSFs. The major areas that need to be considered in competitor analysis in such an approach are:

- Identity of existing/potential competitor.
- Is the competitor direct or indirect?
- What sort of branch/office network do they operate?
- Who are the key people in the competitor firm and in what areas do they work?
- What range of services does the competitor offer?
- In what service areas do they specialize or have the greatest strength?
- What is the composition of their client base?
- Do they specialize in any type of client?
- What is their fee structure and at what levels are fees set?
- How does their fee income break down in terms of service offerings?
- How strong is their competitive position in marketplaces in which we compete?
- What are the competitor firms' major perceived strengths?

- What are their major perceived weaknesses?
- What are the features of their current strategy for development?

Even when PSFs are provided with, or develop, frameworks for analysing competition many professionals seem incapable of systematically collecting competitive intelligence. Many professionals ask me on a regular basis 'where can we find information about our competitors?' or try to convince me that finding the necessary competitive information is impossible. This is, of course, nonsense and there are professional service firms who operate continuous and systematic competitive intelligence activities. Other firms remain naive in terms of analysing competition. At a recent seminar for lawyers a partner in a small firm told me about a Law Society directory of firms that was a mine of competitive information. In discussing the source of the information the partner explained that all participating firms filled in a questionnaire, were included in the directory and received a copy in return. In asking the partner about the reliability of his own firm's disclosures – which turned out to be largely unreliable – and then about the reliability that his firm placed in the directory entries of its competitors in formulating its competitive strategy, the lesson is clear, directory information needs to be externally validated before it can be used in competitive strategy formulation.

However, in spite of the protestations of numerous professionals a large number of sources of competitive information are available:

Published sources: anything written about competition and potential competitors should be collected and analysed. Published sources include books, reports and articles, features, etc., in the newspapers, professional journals and business/management press.

Competitors' sources: competitors, in much the same way as all PSFs (including yours) generally have a lot to tell you directly through brochures, annual reports, recruitment literature, advertisements, press releases, newsletters, etc. This is a particularly fruitful source of information since it enables a good deal of a competitor's strategy to be deduced (advertisement copy and target audience, launch of new services, recruitment of new professionals, etc.).

Interaction sources: professionals in areas of particular services, industries and geographic areas interact between firms on a regular basis. Much competitive information can be collected into its competitive intelligence system, even if this only entails ensuring that all staff fill in intelligence worksheets after such interactive occasions. Further interaction between larger firms also often occurs in terms of family and emotional relationships between staff of competing firms. This can also be a fruitful source of information.

117

Networking sources: all professionals develop informal networks of contacts as a part of their professional lives. Particularly fruitful in networking sources are contacts who are referral sources, e.g. accountants, bank managers, lawyers, etc. These people interact with both you and probably also your competitors and can and do provide useful competitive information.

Client sources: in many professions clients move occasionally from one professional service firm to another, and many clients also use more than one supplier of professional services. In dealing with competitors on a day-to-day basis client sources can provide some of the most important competitive information – how the marketplace perceives the strengths and weaknesses of your competitors.

Direct sources: these are direct services in the sense that information can be obtained direct from your competitors, but indirect in the sense that the competitor believes it is supplying information to someone else. At a simple level this involves getting one of your staff, at their home address, on the mailing list of a competitor. At a more complex level it can involve phoning competitors to ask for quotes, pretending to be a prospective client and asking questions, etc. These activities are legal and can become as complex as is necessary. Ethics do not enter this as a serious issue. I know a large number of firms who regularly collect information in this way; your firm needs to be aware of this before they choose to dismiss this source of competitive intelligence.

It is therefore obvious that information about competitors is available. As with segmentation, however, competitive intelligence does not simply leap out at you. Competitive intelligence systems, even simple worksheet/questionnaire-based approaches, will need time, effort and resource to put together and maintain. As with most other business activities you get nothing for nothing. In the context of competitive intelligence and competitor analysis a quote from Philip Kotler is particularly apposite: 'It has been said that there are three types of companies: those that make things happen, those that watch things happen, and those that wonder what happened'.[8] In order to ensure that your firm is not one of those that wonder what happened, the least that is required is a mechanism for collecting the competitive intelligence and information that is routinely carried around in the heads of most of the staff of all PSFs and feeding this information into the firm's strategic and marketing planning process.

An allied approach to the problem of analysing competition in marketplaces for professional services is that of strategic groups. This is a very simple approach that calls for the identification of all the suppliers of professional services to a particular marketplace and clustering these suppliers into 'strategic groups' of firms. There are many types of bases that can be applied for the purposes of groupings but the most useful, suggested by Aaker are:[9]

- the similarity over time of competitive strategies (i.e. service width, office networks, level of promotion, etc.);
- similarity in firm characteristics (i.e. size, aggressiveness, etc.);
- similarity of assets and skills (e.g. quality image, perceived areas of expertise, etc.).

If some form of strategic group analysis for a given service-market is performed then it is usually possible to identify a number of mobility barriers that work both as barriers to exit for firms within a strategic group and as barriers to entry to alternative strategic groups.[10] This is not to say that PSFs cannot move from one strategic group to another, but there are usually costs and long time periods associated with such moves. Firms in different strategic groups will compete in the marketplace upon different bases and are likely to have different competitive advantages.

The strategic groups concept is a useful way of breaking down competitor analysis into a simple model and can often be achieved in a workable practical form without vast amounts of information or time. It can be particularly useful in professional service marketplaces in which there are large numbers of potential competitors that would make individual analysis of all of them logistically and economically difficult.

One way of starting a strategic groups analysis of a marketplace for professional services that I have found useful in working with PSFs is

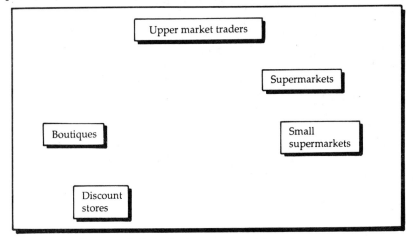

Figure 7.6 *Stereotypical strategic groups model*

to introduce a retailing analogy. In many situations the typical strategic groups model that emerges looks like the one shown in Figure 7.6.

These groupings, in the professional service context, may be seen to have the following profiles:

Upper market traders usually smaller, old established PSFs with something of an 'exclusive' image. Often they have limited office networks but very good informal networks of contacts and referral sources that have been built up and carefully cultivated over a long period. These firms compete openly upon quality, are often seen within the profession as arrogant and have high fee levels, e.g. Cazenoves in stockbroking.

Supermarkets these are usually the largest firms in the profession with the widest office network. They offer a huge range of services without being seen as specialist in any particular service area. These firms compete upon the ability to provide 'one-stop shopping' and also often upon their international arms or network links, e.g. Ove Arup in consulting engineering.

Small supermarkets these usually form the second and third tier of firms in a profession. These are medium-sized firms, who usually wish to emulate the larger firms and therefore offer a wide range of services although often with a smaller office network and weaker international links. The small supermarkets usually attempt to differentiate themselves by offering greater partner accessibility and often lower fees than the supermarkets.

Boutiques these are smaller firms who concentrate upon a specific segment of the marketplace as the main part of their business. They will initially specialize in either a type of service offering or in a specific industry and will be perceived as a leader in this segment by the marketplace. Such firms often have small office networks and tend to concentrate more on individual geographic locations, e.g. Stoy Haywood accountants specializing in franchising.

Discount stores these often make up the bulk of the number of firms in a profession. They are most often locally based small partnerships with relatively limited specialist expertise. These 'general practices' are usually the cheapest and most abundant suppliers in a professional service marketplace although few of them actively and explicitly compete on price, e.g. your local high street solicitor.

This type of strategic groups model can provide a very good starting point for developing a firm's own model of competition in a given professional service marketplace. One of the best things about this model is that it is appealing to non-marketing partners and professionals in professional service firms who seem to grasp quickly the insight that such a strategic groups analysis can give into competitive positions in a marketplace and thus its impact upon the marketing strategies formulated by the firm.

This sort of analysis really lifts off when, having identified rough groups, we begin to ask questions such as: which of these groups are most profitable and have the highest fees; which groups are growing and which shrinking; what are the likely changes in group structure and size over the next three to five years; which groups can be perceived as the 'winners' and 'losers' in this marketplace; what seem to be the critical success factors that differentiate them?

Perhaps the question that has most impact in operationalizing the strategic groups concept and generating immediately recognizable strategic insights is the question 'which group is your firm in?'. It can also be useful to make explicit, and even quantify in rough terms, the type and cost of barriers to mobility that exist, e.g. what are the barriers to leaving the 'boutique' group and entering the 'supermarket' group? How much would it cost us in monetary and human terms to overcome these? How much time is it likely to take to complete such a movement?

This is an invaluable exercise in demonstrating the implications of various strategy options and is often an enlightening and sobering exercise of great value for partners in professional service firms.

References

1 Wind, Y. (1978), 'Firms and advances in segmentation research', *Journal of Marketing Research*, vol. 15, pp. 137–337.
2 Haley, R. I. (1968), 'Benefit segmentation: a decision-oriented research tool', *Journal of Marketing*, vol. 32, pp. 30–35, July.
3 Bonoma, T. V. and Shapiro, B. P. (1983), *Segmenting the Industrial Market*, Lexington, MA: D C Heath.
4 Lynn, S. A. (1986), 'Segmenting a business market for a professional service', *Industrial Marketing Management*, vol. 15, pp. 13–21.
5 Evans, J. R. and Berman, B. (1987), *Marketing* (3rd edn) New York: Macmillan, p. 212.
6 Kotler, P. (1986), *Marketing Management: Analysis, Planning and Control* (5th edn), Englewood Cliffs, NJ: Prentice Hall.
7 Porter, M. E. (1979), 'How competitive forces shape strategy', *Harvard Business Review*, March–April, pp. 137–145.
8 Kotler, P. (1980), 'Strategic planning and the marketing process', *Business* (US) May–June, pp. 2–9.
9 Aaker, D. (1989), *Strategic Market Management* (2nd edn) New York: John Wiley.
10 Porter, M. E. (1980), *Competitive Strategy*, New York: The Free Press.

8 Strategy alternatives

Having completed the strategic marketing audit stage of the planning process we have analysed the present position of the firm in relation to its clients, marketplaces, competitors, environmental forces and its own strategic marketing goals and objectives. This chapter concentrates upon the next step in the planning process, the generation and evaluation of strategy options.

Even if we have managed to persuade our partners and senior managers to take part in the necessary planning activities outlined in this book to date, we are still left with a problem in many firms. As a result of the preceding analysis, and the time and mental effort involved in the strategic marketing audit, many planners expect the 'right' or 'optimal' strategies to simply drop out of the marketing audit.

In reality this rarely, if ever, happens. From this stage of the planning process what is required is the generation of as many strategy options as possible from the audit, and a mechanism for choosing between them. We are looking for a strategy which is potentially capable of not only moving the firm from its current position towards its strategic marketing objectives, but is also the least likely to cause internal implementation problems which often undermine the potential of a strategy. This chapter provides frameworks which are useful in generating strategy options that provide focus and objectivity, as well as a stimulus to planners for this stage in the process. Also provided is a mechanism which can aid planners in building a set of structured criteria which can be used in order to choose one strategy from the various strategy alternatives.

Generic marketing strategy options

In attempting to generate a range of alternative strategies for consideration, in the light of the strategic marketing audit and the long-term marketing goals and objectives of the firm, one of the simplest frameworks that can be utilized is a simple list of generic strategy options. One of the most useful of these simple generic strategy frameworks has been developed by Hofer and Schendel.[1] This framework outlines eight generic strategy alternatives for the consideration of planners.

1 *Test strategy* This strategy option is related to the opening up of new client markets for existing service offerings, e.g. opening a new office in a new geographic market, developing new professional service offerings for existing client markets or even diversification moves in developing new service offerings for new client markets. The test strategy is often seen as a pre-introduction option which focuses primarily upon obtaining market information and testing market reactions to new developments. As such, in some cases this may lead to it being seen as attractive since it can postpone a full-blown strategy selection and implementation. Interestingly, however, in spite of the popularity of 'test marketing' in FMCG markets, this is an option which is rarely used in the professional service context.

2 *Develop strategy* The develop option is most usually associated with service-markets where the potential clients are largely unfamiliar with the benefits of the services being offered. In this strategy market communications are important and play a strong information/educa-tion role for potential clients. The critical focus of this option is creating awareness, knowledge and interaction with potential clients. Differentiation and positioning are usually important in the successful implementation of this option.

3 *Penetrate strategy* This alternative is essentially focused upon gaining market share from competing firms and is often associated with service markets which are relatively mature. This option usually calls for greater investment, particularly in terms of marketing budget, since it entails growing the business and its market share faster than the market growth rate. The adoption and implementation of a penetrate strategy involves a commitment of resource but also, in most cases, a willingness to forgo short-term profitability for longer-term benefits via market share growth.

4 *Maintain strategy* The maintenance strategy option is fairly self-explanatory. It entails making sufficient investment and efforts to hold market share against competitor firms but not to attempt to build market share faster than the general market growth rate. This option usually appears most attractive to firms in mature service markets. Maintenance strategies may involve not only maintaining parity and position against existing competitors but also building barriers to entry, which will make it more difficult and costly for new or alternative suppliers to enter the service-market.

5 *Rebuild strategy* This option involves restoring the competitive position of a firm in a service market after a decline in performance or inroads by competitors, etc. The objective is to regain market position and/or market share in expectation of either market growth in the

future or the possibility of the service-market providing a strategic platform into new and emerging service-markets. This is often seen as a risky strategy since it is often applicable in increasingly competitive service-markets and usually offers no immediate payback in the short term.

6 *Harvest strategy* The focus in this option is upon increasing returns and short-term profitability with little or no regard for the longer-term service-market position. As such, this type of strategy is most often associated with late mature and declining markets in which it may be perceived that the 'market life cycle' gives little hope of long-term or even medium-term prospects. This type of strategy is often adopted in 'cash cow' scenarios where the cash harvested from the service market in the short term is used to fund the development of new services and new markets in other parts of the business.

7 *Divest strategy* In the professional service context, this strategy essentially concerns the freeing up of funds for investment elsewhere in the business through the sale of a business unit, such as an office or a division, i.e. the sale of a recruitment consultancy by a management consultancy group or a fund management business by a stockbroker. This strategy is often applicable to 'problem children' businesses that the firm feels incapable of developing sufficiently or 'dogs' which are unattractive to the firm but may be attractive to some other firm.

8 *Exit strategy* Here the obvious point is to leave the particular service-market completely. In many cases the firm's relationship and advisory obligation to existing clients in that marketplace make a simple 'shutting up shop' approach unattractive and even damaging to other areas of the business. A common approach to exiting a particular service-market is to keep raising fee levels until clients seek alternative suppliers. A more attractive but managerially time-consuming approach may be to arrange for the transfer of clients to a preferred alternative supplier. This may be done simply for the benefit of clients and to protect market image but may also lead to exchange with the new supplier in some way.

There is obviously no 'correct' strategy choice for any given service market situation. Indeed academics are now moving away from viewing the planning process as a search for *the* 'optimal' strategy in any particular scenario. This view will be developed further in Chapter 11. However, the use of even very simple strategy alternative frameworks does force planners to consider a wide range of options, some of which would otherwise be ignored. Consideration of these wider alternatives can in itself provide valuable insight.

One of the problems that I frequently encounter in running planning teams of senior managers and partners is the temptation for them to simply solve all the short-term operating problems that the strategic audit uncovers, and treat this as strategy generation and selection. I have a good deal of sympathy with this temptation, professionals are, by and large, promoted upon their ability to solve short-term problems – be they client or internal operating problems. Once promoted into the ranks of the partnership, however, they are suddenly asked to stop thinking about solving short-term operating problems and start thinking 'strategically' which is usually something they have never been asked to do before, and for which they have often received little or no training. However, simply solving the operating problems highlighted in the marketing audit does not constitute a strategy.

It is in this context that two other widely-known models can prove to be useful in forcing planners to move away from the temptation to solve the short-term problems and to take an informed and objective strategic direction in the longer term. The first of these frameworks is Ansoff's product–market matrix.[2]

Ansoff's matrix is concerned primarily with the directions of the firm or 'growth vectors', rather than the explicit nature of the strategy required to move the firm in that direction (Figure 8.1). As such it is a useful framework to employ in conjunction with others. This is useful in deciding upon the desired direction of the firm's growth. Subsequent frameworks such as the previous generic strategy options or the following frameworks are useful in looking more specifically at which particular strategies may be appropriate for achieving the desired growth vector.

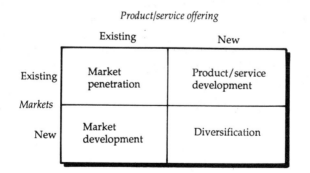

Figure 8.1 *Product–market matrix*

In situations where a firm either wishes to remain serving its existing client base with its existing service offering or is constrained in some way from moving in any new direction, then the obvious growth direction that is appropriate is market penetration. The generation and consideration of strategy alternatives can therefore be narrowed to those that will best provide market share growth in existing service-markets.

Where the growth potential of market penetration is seen to be unattractive then a firm will usually decide to move in one of two directions. It can either decide that its basic strength lies in its relationship with its existing client base in which case it may seek to add to and modify its range of services on offer to its clients, or it may be that the firm is more of a specialist in a type of service, in which case it may be more appropriate to look for new client segments and markets that may also benefit from this service specialization.

The final option in the product–market matrix is also the most inherently risky – diversification. This option has proven to be an extremely dangerous and largely unrewarding direction for growth in manufacturing sectors, and is potentially even more hazardous in the professional service context. In many ways this growth vector should be seen as a 'last resort' to be considered only when the possibilities and potential of the other three generic growth directions have been fully considered.

Having decided, in the light of the strategic marketing audit, the direction of the future growth of the firm, then a second model from Harvard's Michael Porter may usefully move the strategy generation phase of the planning process into more specific terms.[3] Porter's generic strategy model (Figure 8.2), as with his competitive forces model, appears to be disingenuously simple.

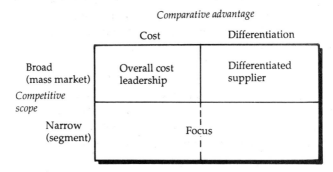

Figure 8.2 *Generic strategies*

The Porter approach is more specific than the Ansoff model. In Porter's view there are three basic generic strategy options that need to be evaluated by firms before selecting a single strategy to implement. First there is an overall cost leadership strategy. In this option the firm adopts a broad competitive scope (i.e. a mass marketing approach) and therefore produces a relatively standard service offering designed to appeal to the greatest number of potential clients, but enjoys a cost advantage over its main competitors and usually passes this unit cost saving on to the client in terms of lower fees, and this forms the basis of the firm's competitive thrust.

The second option is that of becoming a broad differentiated supplier where the mass market coverage approach is adopted but the competitive strategy is based not upon fee levels but upon another base of differentiation, e.g. office network, international connections, technical quality, service quality, branding, etc.

The final strategy is actually two options. The focus strategy means that the firm will adopt a segment based approach, usually either upon client sector specialization or service offering specialization. In terms of competitive strategy and comparative advantage, there are the two different options of cost-based leadership in the particular service-market segment or some other differentiation strategy.

The Porter generic strategy model is obviously an adjunct to his analysis of factors affecting competition in marketplaces. The basic thesis is that having analysed a service marketplace, identifying both the factors affecting competition and the competitive strategies adopted by the major firms, then a firm can choose a strategy from the model that will allow it to build a defensible competitive position, i.e. it is not too directly in 'toe to toe' competition with another major player in the marketplace. Porter also sounds a note of warning with his analysis. He suggests that the generic strategy options are mutually exclusive and that 'stuck in the middle firms', i.e. firms pursuing more than one of the generic strategy options, will be the least successful in any service marketplace. It is, however, possible for different units within the firm, i.e. departments, individual offices, client service groups, etc. to pursue different strategies within a single firm as long as their client bases do not overlap.

Porter's generic strategy options are useful in focusing the minds of planners upon two of the critical dimensions of strategy formulation: market segmentation and competitive differentiation. However, this leaves partners and senior managers within PSFs with a strategy alternative that they may wish to pursue, e.g. to become a broad differentiated supplier, but without any clearer idea of how to differentiate themselves from their competitors. In working with PSFs upon the issue of competitive differentiation it has proven useful to put together frameworks of potential bases for differentiation to be evaluated by planners.

At the simplest level it is possible to think in terms of the potential for differentiation presented by the marketing mix (Figure 8.3).

Marketing mix variable	Possible differentiation bases
Service offering (product)	Technical quality Service quality
Fees (price)	Low/high fees Countertrade vs cash Project vs standard costing
Communications (promotion)	Firm image Service branding
Distribution (place)	Office network International connections

Figure 8.3 *Marketing mix differentiation bases*

Another approach which is particularly useful in illustrating the problems associated with marketing a service, and that fits in well with the strategy generation phase of the planning process, is a service characteristics matrix (Figure 8.4).

Service characteristic	Strategy options	Potential differentiation
Service intangibility	Make more tangible	Focus on service provider Add tangible elements
	Make less tangible	Firm image Branding
Inseparability of production and consumption	Increase separation	Off site service provision Front office/operations split
	Decrease separation	On site service provision Staff placements with client
Perishability of services	Manage demand	Differential fee schedules Limit client base
	Manage supply	Partner accessibility Office hours and days
Heterogeneity of services	Service standardization	Technical quality assurance
	Technology utilization	Systems and administration quality
	Recruitment and training	Technical service excellence service quality

Figure 8.4 *Service characteristic differentiation bases*

These two frameworks for potential bases of differentiation give planners in PSFs a range of differentiating factors to consider, most of which are otherwise easily missed in the strategic planning process. The PSF can consider each of the potential differentiation bases open to them and can evaluate each in terms of (i) how the major competitors are perceived and differentiated in the particular service marketplace under examination, (ii) as a result of the internal situation analysis, what would have to happen within the firm to deliver each differentiated service into the marketplace, (iii) which of the potential bases of differentiation would be most readily perceived and recognized by our target market and (iv) which of the bases of differentiation would add value and increase perceived benefits for clients.

Evaluating strategy alternatives

Having forced those involved in strategic and marketing planning to consider long-term strategy alternatives, rather than rushing off to solve short-term operating problems, and provided frameworks for generating strategic options to ensure that every strategic avenue is considered, partners and managers are still left with the problem of 'how do we know which strategy to adopt?' Again I find myself in sympathy with professionals. Deciding upon the medium and long-term strategy of a firm is a big responsibility and the cost of making a 'wrong' choice could be the survival of the firm itself – particularly in the increasingly hostile business environments that most PSFs face. Faced with such responsibility, even using the frameworks available, there is still a large range of strategy options to choose between in most service-market situations. The initial reaction of most planners is to do nothing, to put off making a choice by claiming to need more information about markets, competitors, costs, etc. before selecting a strategy. Conversely, another risk-reducing approach commonly used by PSFs is to try to come up with a composite of two or three strategy options – the approach that Porter has described as 'stuck in the middle'.

While having some sympathy with PSFs on this point, however, putting off the selection of a strategy or diluting a strategic choice by trying to do everything, is an abdication of responsibility and likely to be damaging. Indeed, many analysts and writers believe that the actual strategy adopted by an organization is largely unimportant in terms of growth and profitability, etc. What *is* vital is that a single clear strategy is adopted and implemented, not the particular detail or type of strategy itself.

In addition to this it is possible to use an existing strategic management approach to develop a customized tool for use within a PSF that will provide clear guidelines and recommendations for choosing between strategy alternatives. This tool is an evolutionary version of the well-known GE 'Business Screen' and links the Porter work with internal factors affecting the strengths and weaknesses of the firm *vis-à-vis* a service market and a strategy alternative. This hybrid tool for evaluating strategy alternatives is known as business position assessment (BPA).

In simple terms the business position assessment approach forces PSF planners to consider two critical question: 'How attractive is a particular service-market strategy to our firm? and 'What competitive position can we take in this service market with this strategy?' The particular strength of this approach to evaluating alternative market strategies is that it can be customized easily to reflect the reality of the criteria that are applied within a firm in evaluating investment decisions.

The first stage in business position assessment is therefore the building of a set of rating scales for both market attractiveness and competitive position. The rating criteria are best arrived at through a planning team 'brainstorming' session. The first question to be addressed is 'just what is it about a particular market segment and marketing strategy that would make it attractive or unattractive to the key decision makers in this firm at this point in time?' There are likely to be a number of rational economic factors which will usually affect how attractive a particular strategy is to a firm that may include:

- the size of the potential market;
- the likely market growth rate;
- the position and strength of existing competitors;
- the likelihood of new entrants;
- the degree of difficulty involved in servicing market needs;
- the 'fit' with the firm's existing strategy;
- the applicability of the firm's existing resources, both human and systems, in meeting the needs of the markets.

There are also likely to be additional, more specific, criteria that are both explicitly and implicitly applied to investment and strategic decisions within the firm. In my experience of using this in planning teams, these criteria have ranged from 'we will not enter a service marketplace unless we believe it will grow at a compound rate of 10 per cent or above for the next five years' – in a firm that was driven by an overall strategy of fast growth above all else in the medium term, to a firm that was interested in diversifying away from its traditional core business and therefore had 'potential for providing a strategic platform into other service markets' as one of the most important criteria in evaluating market attractiveness. Obviously in providing a list of criteria that evaluates market attractiveness for a particular firm the backgrounds, experiences and even the 'hobby-horses' of the key decision makers and relevant committee members have to be considered. It is precisely these senior managers and partners whose support and commitment is initially needed to have any chance of implementing a strategy, and in whose hands the resource decisions for implementing a strategy ultimately lie.

While a large number of criteria may be generated by a planning team, in most PSF situations not all of the criteria will be equal in terms of importance and planners should therefore attempt to 'negotiate' a rough weighting for each of the criteria. Some planners may be able to generate lists of twenty or more criteria, however in most situations five or six weighted criteria are usually sufficient to produce a robust, and more importantly roughly accurate, set of criteria that will largely dictate how the firm will evaluate just how attractive a particular market segment and marketing strategy is to them (Figure 8.5).

Rating criteria – market attractiveness	Weight
1 Stable demand 2 Limited competition 3 Fee sensitivity 4 Open up additional service markets 5 Large enough (over £1m potential demand)	.30 .20 .20 .15 .15
	100

Figure 8.5 *Business position assessment – typical market attractiveness criteria*

The second part of the business position assessment approach is to produce a similar list of rating criteria that are likely to be used within the firm in order to assess the attractiveness and acceptability of the competitive position that the firm can establish in a particular service marketplace, i.e. answering the questions 'how competitive can we be in this segment?' and 'what are the likely results we can expect for the firm?'

Issues that are often considered important in professional service firms in evaluating the attractiveness of likely business position include:

- the market share that could be achieved with clients;
- the lack of vulnerability to competitive attack;
- the breadth of service offerings needed;
- the stability of the competitive position achievable;
- the likely impact upon cross selling opportunities.

Again, within individual PSFs some 'irrational' criteria may also be implicitly used in investment and growth decisions which will usually reflect the attitudes and beliefs of the key decision makers within the firm. One firm I have worked with was very conservative in its approach to entering new service markets and thus in assessing the position that the firm could take in a particular service market. In this firm the most important criteria (Figure 8.6) related to the potential to provide stable fee income, and avoiding being a 'pioneer' of brand new markets in order to reduce the risk inherent in creating 'emerging markets' and incurring costs normally associated with producing generic service awareness in new markets.

Rating criteria – competitive position	Weight
1 Stable fee income	.30
2 Not a market pioneer	.30
3 Invulnerable to competitive attack	.20
4 Potential longevity of position	.10
5 Limited additional recruitment required	
	100

Figure 8.6 *Business position assessment – typical competitive position criteria*

As with the market attractiveness part of BPA the competitive position criteria should be 'negotiated' within the planning team and appropriate rankings applied to each of the criteria.

Many firms during the strategy formulation process implicitly and explicitly consider the firm's likely and potential competitive position. One of the most common 'shorthands' for denoting competitive position in a particular marketplace has been outlined by Jain.[4] This widely used classification of potential competitive positions proposes six categories.

1 *Dominant* Where the firm is a market leader and can largely control the strategies and actions of its competitors as well as

having a wide degree of choice in its own future strategies and actions in the service marketplace.

2   *Strong*   The firm is able to take a competitive stance that is not dependent upon existing competitor suppliers and is able to maintain a long-term position in the face of competitor strategies and actions.

3   *Favourable*   The firm possesses strengths which are potentially exploitable in given market conditions and has an above average ability to improve position *vis-à-vis* competitors.

4   *Tenable*   The firm has sufficient potential and strengths to warrant staying in the service market and is able to maintain its position although unlikely to improve greatly and tends to be only marginally profitable.

5   *Weak*   The firm's performance is unsatisfactory but it has some strengths and capabilities which may lead to improvement. This is inherently a short-term position in that the firm will wish to either improve its competitive position or to exit the service marketplace.

6   *Untenable*   The firm has an unsatisfactory performance and few potential strengths or capabilities that may potentially lead to dramatic improvement.

Having constructed two sets of weighted rating scales for the firm in terms of market attractiveness and competitive position we now have a basic tool for evaluating marketing strategies. During the strategy formulation phase of the marketing planning process PSFs, in considering the strategic options open to them, will usually very quickly be able to focus their efforts by discounting the strategy alternatives that simply do not seem viable for the firm at that time. In reality firms will generally only need to consider two or three strategy alternatives in depth with the rating criteria generated. Planners can simply evaluate and score each of the strategy alternatives on each of the criteria and produce weighted scores in terms of market attractiveness (Figure 8.7(a)) and competitive position (Figure 8.7(b)) for each of the strategy alternatives.

The strategic options under active consideration at this stage are listed at the top of the diagnostic and then the criteria generated and weighted earlier are applied to each of the strategy alternatives producing first a raw score (usually out of ten or 100) depending upon how that particular option measures up against that particular criteria, and then a weighted score (the raw score × the weighting of the criteria). The weighted scores can then be calculated for each of the strategy options in terms of market attractiveness and competitive position.

Market attractiveness criteria	Weight	Strategy options					
		1 Score	Wt Score	2 Score	Wt Score	3 Score	Wt Score
1							
2							
3							
4							
5							
		Total		Total		Total	

(a)

Competitive position criteria	Weight	Strategy options					
		1 Score	Wt Score	2 Score	Wt Score	3 Score	Wt Score
1							
2							
3							
4							
5							
		Total		Total		Total	

(b)

Figure 8.7 *Business position assessment proforma*

With these weighted scores it may be useful to plot each strategy option's total on a business strategy position matrix as illustrated in Figure 8.8.

By simply positioning each of the strategies on the matrix, planners can build up a picture of which are likely to be the most and least attractive of the strategy alternatives open to the firm. It can therefore provide clear guidelines, based upon the real criteria of assessment used within the firm, of which strategies are the most likely to appeal to key decision makers and committees within the firm and thus achieve the resources and, more importantly, the commitment and support of

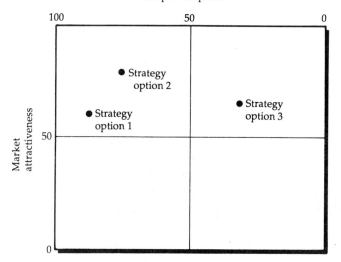

Figure 8.8 *Business strategy position matrix*

the senior managers and partners that is vital for the successful implementation of any strategy.

The business position assessment approach can therefore allow planners to make an objective, informed and realistic evaluation of the strategy alternatives that are open to them. Having decided which option to pursue, however, it is important that planners do not simply assume that all the necessary evaluation of the strategy chosen has been completed. One approach to the continued evaluation of the strategic option adopted by the firm is the use of a questioning approach such as that developed by George Day in Canada.[5] These 'tough questions' which planners must continually pose and answer at each stage of the further development and implementation of the marketing strategy are:

1 *Competitive advantage* Does this strategy allow the firm to develop or capitalize upon a competitive advantage which we can sustain in the medium term?
2 *Validity* On what assumptions is the success of the strategy based, are they realistic and can they be validated?
3 *Feasibility* Does the firm realistically have the skills, resources and commitment to make this strategy actually work?
4 *Consistency* Do the elements of the strategy actually hang together? e.g. does the pricing strategy make sense in a specialist, high quality service strategy?

5 *Vulnerability* What are the risks that the firm faces with implementing this strategy and what contingency plans can the firm make?

6 *Financial desirability* As the strategy unfolds and the tactical actions in implementation are planned and costed, does the strategy still make financial sense for the firm?

Every professional service firm, even the most marketing sophisticated, would benefit from the constant questioning of their business and marketing strategies along the above lines. The answering of these questions is a painful and potentially fruitful discipline which will ensure that plans and strategies are thoroughly evaluated and can increase the likelihood of plans and strategies being accepted and resourced by the firm and actually becoming a reality that is delivered into the marketplace.

References

1 Hofer, C. and Schendel, D. (1984), *Strategy Formulation: Analytical Concepts*, West.

2 Ansoff, H. I. (1968), *Corporate Strategy*, London: Penguin, p. 99.

3 Porter, M. E. (1981), *Competitive Strategy*, New York: The Free Press.

4 Jain, S. C. (1989), *Marketing Planning and Strategy* (3rd edn), Cincinnati: South Western, p. 262.

5 Day, G. S. (1986), 'Tough questions for developing strategies', *The Journal of Business Strategy*, Winter, pp. 60–68.

Appendix   Strategic marketing audit worksheets

1 The market

Focus	Analyse	Objective
Client needs and buying factors	Client priorities in the needs met through purchase. Client group differences	Emphasize client needs not services offered and differences between client segments
Services and clients	Group services by common needs satisfied and clients or markets by common characteristics	Create service offerings and client definitions reflecting marketplace not internal professional operations
Main services	Identify the key services for each client group/market	Establish client group/market differences in service priorities
Marketing priorities and critical success factors	Evaluation of most important marketing mix element for each client group/market. What do the 'winners' get right?	Establish relative effectiveness of marketing mix variables and competitive requirements
Firm priorities	Compare each match of service offering and client group to – potential competitiveness – attractiveness of the segment – match with internal requirements	Isolate areas of high and low priority for the firm and niche gaps and opportunities in segments
Market sizing and shares	Potential market size and growth rates and shares taken by competitors	Place values on segments

| Competitors | Evaluate direct and indirect competitors, entrants and leavers, major competitors characteristics | Identify competitive position |
| Marketing environment | Evaluate likely impact of broad changes in markets, legislation, economics, etc. | Put planning in broad business context |

SWOT and strategies

2 Service offering strategy

Focus	Analyse	Objective
Competitive performance	In each client group/ market segment how well does our service offering meet clients' needs compared to competitors	Identify gaps in matching services to high priority client needs and gaps in competitors' offerings
Service dimensions	For the critical markets and service offerings, how well do we perform in service specifications, service breadth and service	Concentrate upon differentiation potential of service offerings and not upon the basic generic service offering
Service lines	For critical client needs and service offerings where do we stand against market standards and market leaders. Where are specific service gaps and deficiencies	Develop list of shortfalls and actions needed to remedy

SWOT and strategies

3 Distribution strategy

Focus	Analyse	Objective
Office location	Client base and service offerings related to geography	Take broad view of appropriate location
Service location	Business done in office and in client premises. Satellite service branches?	View opportunities for client satisfaction via delivery of service
Competitors' strategy	Where are our major competitors in each segment based? Where do they deliver service?	Compare our distribution strategy with competitors
Partner/staff accessibility	How accessible are staff in our offices – physical, communications	Enforce view of accountability as critical distribution variable
Office accessibility	How easy is it for clients to visit	Emphasize client service quality criteria
Physical surroundings	Evidence of physical environment as a client cue	View physical evidence of surroundings from client viewpoint

SWOT and strategies

4 Marketing communications strategy

Focus	Analyse	Objective
Corporate/brand positioning	Identify client and market perceptions of our firm and key competitors	Identify broad communications tasks

Decision making units	Within each market segment/client group, model the DMU, identify roles adopted and relevant messages and media	Isolate DMU targets for communications and messages required
External influences	Within market segments/client groups identify major influence sources e.g. referral agencies and our standing compared to competitors	Isolate influencer targets for communications and messages required
Media	Within each segment/ client group identify available media of communication and compare effectiveness for DMU members and influencers	Take broad view of communications media
Media performance	Compare our effectiveness in using each medium and expenditure with key competitors	Relate effort to market share and isolate areas for development

---

SWOT and strategies

---

5 Pricing strategy

Focus	*Analyse*	*Objective*
Service pricing	Within each segment compare service fee levels to key competitors and our price position in the segment	Identify service fee level positioning
Market pricing	Compare our fee level position by segment with key competitors and across our total markets	Identify market price positions and relationships with market share

Fee trends	Examine service fee level trends over past years and expected future movement	Identify risers and fallers
Value	Compare perceived quality, fee level position and market share for our firm and key competitors	Break the 'low fee = high volume' perceptions and look for positioning anomalies
Fee structures	For key service offerings compare the component fee structures with key competitors	Compare our fee strategy with competitors and its implications for market share
Fee awareness and communications	How sensitive are client groups to fees? Compare against competitors' fee information given to clients before and after service performed	Identify price-sensitive segments and fee structure and levels as source of communication and potential differentiation

SWOT and strategies

6 Summary of audit

Focus	Analyse	Objective
Life cycle and competitive position	Life cycle stage and competitive position in each segment	Prioritize market segments and niches
Market summary	Across segments analyse life cycle stages, value, priority service offerings, marketing mix requirements	Collate market and competitive positioning
Market priorities	Across segments analyse our market share and fee income projections, chances of success and priorities	Choose priority market targets

Critical success factors	In priority segments what do we have to get right to succeed?	Specific action list
Marketing objectives	In priority segments, the key marketing objectives and how they relate to market share and fee income forecasts	Isolate major market goals
Strategy summary	Reduce to key strategies for each segment and build matrix of segments and marketing strategies	Reduce ideas to high-priority strategies and model required programme for marketing mix across segments
Competitive reactions	Evaluate likely responses of competitors to visible strategies	Identify risks and vulnerabilities
Tactics	Break strategies for segments into lists of tactical actions and identify professionals responsible	Specific action lists
Cost analysis	Evaluate costs of strategies through segments	P & L by segment

Overall marketing plan for firm

Part Four
Marketing Communications

While promotion is only one of the four 'Ps' that are classically seen as constituting the marketing mix, it is the area that has initially attracted the greatest amount of interest from professionals. It is also the area in which professional service firms have received, and paid for, most advice from consultancies in the form of public relations, graphic design, corporate identity and advertising agencies.

In many senses promotion or marketing communications is the most visible area of marketing activity both within and outside professional service firms. The proliferation of new glossy brochures, sophisticated logos, myriad press releases, and three-colour press advertising campaigns have achieved more in terms of raising the profile of marketing communications within the professions than in terms of changing potential client attitudes and raising name awareness in target markets in most firms.

The high profile of marketing communications, which also forms the bulk of most marketing spend within professional service firms, has also served to perpetuate and entrench many of the myths about marketing that were outlined earlier. This book attempts to rectify the apparent imbalance in the perceptions of most professionals about the role and importance of marketing communications *vis-à-vis* the other three elements of the marketing mix and strategic marketing.

The two chapters in this part focus upon three elements of the marketing communications mix in particular: advertising, particularly in terms of planning an advertising campaign; personal selling by the professional as a critical part of the client purchase decision process; and corporate or firm image, with a consideration of the role that public relations can and should play in the marketing communications efforts of professional service firms.

9 Marketing communications and advertising

If it were possible to write a book on professional services marketing without a section concerning marketing communications, then I would gladly do so. The prevailing typology of marketing as 'advertising and selling' with its allied ignorance of the nature of marketing, causes professional services marketers more problems than anything else.[1] A book containing nothing about external marketing communications may serve to send some signals about the true nature of marketing, however it would omit an area that does play a role in marketing, and one in which the greatest amount of academic research has been undertaken.

Much of the misconception surrounding marketing stems from the original relaxation of professional regulations concerning promotion in the accounting, legal, engineering and medical professions. The 'hype' surrounding these events in the professional press at the time of the relaxation of professional regulations served to confuse the terms advertising and marketing in the minds of most professionals. Since advertising is, almost by definition, the most highly visible element of most marketing programmes this mistake on the part of professionals, at least initially, is understandable.

In the large majority of firms, marketing communications activities account for the bulk of the marketing budget. In spite of this, most professional firms believe themselves to have been largely unsuccessful in their marketing communications efforts. In many cases this is caused by a combination of overambitious goals, lack of specific targetting, unclear messages and small budgets. Marketers have some difficulty with marketing communications *vis-à-vis* professionals within their firm since almost every professional seems to implicitly feel that they know something about the subject. This is a widespread personality trait amongst all professionals that is usually manifested at least to the degree that a professional will feel competent and qualified to be able to evaluate advertising campaigns, direct-mail campaigns, brochures, newsletters, logos, etc. Most professional service marketers would be extremely grateful if professionals would recognize that, while their personal opinion of brochure layout, advertisement copy or print style on direct mailings may have some personal validity, they are not usually a member of the audience for which the communications message, vehicle, media, etc. have been chosen and designed and that their personal opinion, whatever it might be, does not influence the success or failure of a promotional campaign. For such professionals, reading these two chapters on marketing communications for professional services might well be the kindest thing you have ever done for your marketing manager, consultant or partner.

The marketing communications mix

If you can remember as far back as Chapter 2 then you may recall that marketing programmes are often defined as having four component parts, the classical '4 Ps' of marketing. One of these four elements is communication (or promotion as it appears in the 4 Ps framework). Marketing communications is itself a mix of four essential elements:

Advertising   any form of non-personal communication about a professional service firm and its service offerings that is sponsored by the firm or on the firm's behalf.
Personal selling   personal communication with existing or prospective client(s) for the purpose of generating fees.
Publicity   non-personal communications regarding a firm or its services that contain commercially significant views or favourable presentation in any media that is not sponsored by the firm or its agents.
Sales promotion   any activity or material that is not advertising, publicity or personal selling that acts as an inducement to referral sources and/or directly to existing and potential clients.

These four communications mix elements comprise the professional service marketer's armoury for communicating with clients, potential clients and referral sources in order to directly or indirectly help create exchanges that may result in greater fee income for the firm.

Advertising

For many years in both the USA and Europe the work on professional services marketing and the focus of most interest in the area centred upon advertising and its relevance, applicability and likely long-term impact upon the professions. Even after the relaxation of regulations concerning some types of marketing communications vehicles and messages, some of these arguments surrounding advertising and the professions remain. The main arguments in this debate are discussed at length in the marketing literature (Bloom, 1977; Stafford, 1988)[2] and while interesting, do not directly impact upon the content of this book.

In considering the role that advertising can play in the business development activities of professional service firms, professionals themselves seem to take extreme and opposing views. Some professionals, having viewed the importance of advertising in the marketing strategies of financial services companies and many other service businesses, take the view that advertising is an essential part of any marketing strategy and that advertising campaigns can effectively sell the service offerings of a PSF. Others have taken the view that advertising in the context of professional services can achieve very little, has no impact upon potential clients and is largely a waste of money. As with most such dichotomous arguments there are elements of validity in either argument with the truth lying somewhere in the middle. In the light of these extreme positions it is worth considering exactly what advertising can and cannot achieve in the context of professional services.

Advertising campaigns can:

1 Create an awareness of a firm's name, its service offerings and areas of expertise which *may* lead to potential client interest and/or action.
2 Aid the establishment or enhancement of an image of the PSF in the marketplace.
3 Enhance the confidence of existing clients in the firm and its service offerings.
4 Provide the cheapest way of reaching a large number of potential clients with a marketing communications message.
5 Help to position the firm in the minds of existing and potential clients and differentiate it from its competitors.

All of these are possible consequences of an advertising campaign but only if the campaign is properly planned, targeted, designed and executed, with sufficient budget and over an appropriate length of time. Even in these 'ideal' circumstances, however, there are a large number of things that an advertising campaign alone cannot achieve.

Advertising campaigns cannot:

1 Sell the services of a professional service firm.
2 Create a corporate identity.
3 Communicate long or complex messages to potential clients.
4 Answer potential client queries.

The most important and erroneous implicit benefit of advertising, as viewed by many 'pro-advertising' professionals, is that advertising alone can sell the services that the firm offers.

This is not, never has been, and never will be true. In many cases professionals would like this to be true since it would largely absolve them of any responsibility for the marketing of their firm's service.

If advertising is to be useful in the professional service context as an integral part of a marketing strategy then it is absolutely essential that advertising campaigns are carefully and thoroughly planned. While to non-marketing professionals advertising may seem to be primarily a creative exercise, the critical prerequisite components for the success of any advertising campaign have nothing, or very little, to do with creativity.

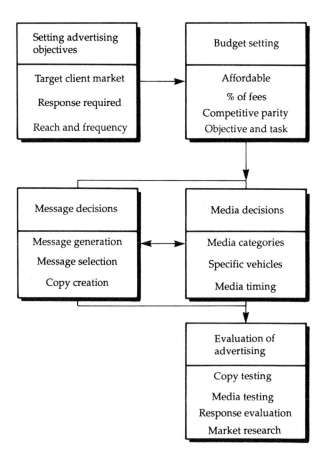

Figure 9.1 *Advertising campaign management process*

The major decisions in planning any advertising campaign for a professional service firm are summarized in Figure 9.1. Each stage is now discussed in more detail.

Setting advertising objectives

The first decision that is faced in planning an advertising campaign is the specific target audience for the campaign. This is a critical decision to the success of any campaign and yet this is a decision which firms often fail to address and make specific in their marketing communications activities. Failing to make an explicit and and specific statement of the target audience for any marketing communications campaign is likely to dilute that campaign's effectiveness. This may be likened to taking a scattergun/blunderbus approach to directing marketing communications rather than using telescopic sights on a hunting rifle to direct messages at specific targets. The latter which is likely to be far more effective in terms of achieving desired communications objectives and efficient in terms of the use of invariably scarce marketing budget.

The importance of careful target audience selection obviates the necessity of some explicit strategic marketing plan. Even a rudimentary strategic marketing plan should make explicit the market segments attractive to the firm and the target areas for focused business development activities. Simple market analysis of the key target markets should make clear to the planners of the advertising campaign the likely target audiences. Given the widespread differences between the activities and clients of professional service firms in the UK, the specific target audience for an advertising campaign may be potential or existing clients, it may be made up of individual consumers, types of organization or even the general public, it may be buyers of professional services, influencers, or even referral sources. Explicit and specific choices need to be made to identify the target audience that will best fulfil the marketing objectives of the strategic marketing plan.

✎ Response required

Having selected a target audience for the advertising campaign, it is also necessary to specify a goal, or even multiple goals, that the campaign is to achieve with the target audience. This goal is usually framed in terms of desired response in the targetted audience. The more specific and limited the required response of a campaign, the easier response is to measure and generally the more effective the campaign. The obvious answer to the question of response required in most partners' eyes seems to be turning the target audience into clients or, for the more moderate, getting our existing clients to buy additional services. Advertising campaigns are tools that may be useful for informing, creating visibility, enhancing image, changing attitudes and helping to cause clients and potential clients to take initial actions. Campaigns that are planned to achieve the communication of information, and visibility objectives such as name awareness, image awareness, etc. are much more likely to be successful than campaigns that attempt to achieve changes in attitude or to affect target audience behaviour. As discussed in Chapter 3 the buying process for professional services for both consumers and organizations is a lengthy and complex process. The target audience, and subsegments of the target audience may be in any one of the stages of buying behaviour. Thus in designing campaigns that have objectives set in terms of influencing target audience behaviour, these objectives are far more likely to be achievable if set in terms of moving target audiences from one stage in the buying process to the next, rather than in terms of moving target audiences through the entire process. It is obviously important in designing such campaigns that the buyer state of the target audience (or the most important part of it) is examined in the market analysis stage of the strategic marketing planning process or made known to the market communicator through some other means.

Consider the case of a small civil engineering practice that specializes in industrial production units for high technology industries. An advertising campaign objective of 'Raising awareness of the firm's name from 5 per cent to 15 per cent of architectural practices located in Scotland, and raising awareness of the firm's primary service offering specialism in high technology production construction from 1 per cent to 7 per cent in the same target audience' is far more likely to lead to a targetted, effective and efficient advertising campaign and is more likely to achieve its explicit and achievable objectives than a campaign for the same firm that has the aim of 'getting us more clients in our field'. Such specific advertising objectives not only allow the firm to evaluate the success of a campaign but also give much more specific guidelines for the design of the campaign itself.

Reach and frequency

With a specified target audience and explicit advertising objectives it is obviously necessary to make a decision, based upon knowledge of the target market and the specific response required, as to the reach (number of people exposed to your advertising message) and frequency (number of exposures to your advertising message) that may be needed to create the desired response in a sufficient number of the target market to achieve strategic marketing objectives.

In the above example of the civil engineering firm it is likely that the reach and frequency necessary to achieve the distinct objectives of name awareness and service specialization awareness will be different. Name awareness is a relatively early stage in the organizational purchasing process and thus in order to achieve desired strategic marketing goals, the civil engineering firm may require a reach of 200 firms of architects to become aware of their name. Awareness of a specific offering and specialist expertise is information that will be acquired by architects later in the purchasing process and thus the reach required to meet strategic marketing targets may only be fifty firms of architects. Similarly, the frequency required for name awareness may only be one or two exposures to advertisements featuring the firm's name prominently, while awareness of specialization, a much more complex image requiring the absorption of a lot more information by architects, may take five or six exposures over a longer period, perhaps in different forms.

Budget setting

Setting communications budgets, or even getting communications budgets in many firms, is a difficult, time-consuming and often heartbreaking experience. In most professional service firms this relies less upon the rational decision-making techniques that may be used in other industries and more upon strength of personality, political manoeuvring and even overt use of organizational power.

In an ideal situation, having made the decisions relating to setting advertising objectives, a budget allocation is made that is sufficient to reasonably achieve the objectives of the advertising campaign. This 'ideal' situation, which is usually referred to as the 'objective and task' method of budget determination, tends to happen only in larger firms, in situations in which the campaign is to be only a very small part of the overall marketing budget. In most cases the rational and logical situation of deciding what you need to do with a campaign and then allocating sufficient funds to achieve that goal does not exist. In fact, in most professional service firms the reverse is true. This method of budget determination, which marketing academics refer to as the 'affordable' method, simply means that the partners, on the basis of projected fee income (usually last year's fee income plus or minus a few per cent for adjustments), allocate a purely arbitrary (and usually small) sum of money for marketing communications. It is then the responsibility of whoever undertakes communications activities to design campaigns and develop reasonable advertising objectives within the budgetary constraints.

In some other situations budgets may be determined by methods which lie somewhere between these two extremes. The most common of these budget determination 'techniques' is 'competitive parity', where a firm will prepare advertising budgets that they believe match those of their closest competitors. This approach is normally used in firms that are relatively marketing unsophisticated and who see both marketing and advertising as essentially defensive responses to market conditions. An alternative budget determination method is 'percentage of fees', where firms have evolved a simple ratio for marketing budgets of a certain percentage of fee income per year. It is often felt that the percentage of fees method offers an inducement to marketers to increase the fee income of the firm. This approach is more often used by professional service firms to determine the entire marketing budget rather than the advertising budget. In the UK, marketing budgets determined through this method usually represent between 1 and 3 per cent of total fee income.

The 'nitty gritty' stages of planning an advertising campaign are related to two decision areas: message and media. These decisions are obviously not mutually exclusive and discrete, and they are therefore presented as parallel and interrelated decision stages in the model indicated in Figure 9.1.

Message decisions

While the marketer may be explicitly aware of the message that is required to be received by the target audience in order to achieve the desired objective of an advertising campaign, it is obvious that this essential message may be received by targets in a number of different guises. It is therefore helpful to consider the major alternative messages that may possibly be sent and that will potentially result in the target audience interpreting and receiving the desired message. This distinction between messages sent and messages received may be significant as communications theory suggests that messages are encoded by the sender (the message designer for the advertising campaign), sent to the target audience via some media (that is an imperfect channel of communication since the target audience are also subject to other messages from other senders) who decode and receive the message on the basis of their own knowledge and experience[3] (see Figure 9.2).

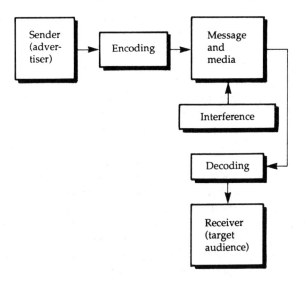

Figure 9.2 *The marketing communications process*
Adapted from Kotler (1985), Marketing Management *(5th edn), Prentice-Hall, p. 605*

It is therefore helpful to generate a number of potential messages that may be received in the desired way by the target audience. In a perfect world the marketer would know which kind of message is most likely to be received in the desired way through exhaustive market research, testing and analysis. In most professional service situations, however, this is very much a judgement call.

Kotler and Bloom suggest a framework for generating messages based upon the appeal to the target audience.[4]

1 *Rational messages* aimed at passing information to the target audience that is usually presented as in their interest. Such messages often emphasize quality, value, etc. to targets.
2 *Emotional messages* these attempt to evoke some emotion in the target audience that will move the potential client to the desired stage of the purchasing process. Common emotional appeals use humour, fear, pride, etc. to achieve this goal.
3 *Moral messages* these are usually directed at feelings of 'right' and 'wrong' that may be used by the target audience and these may often have a commanding or righteous tone.

I would add to this list a fourth type of message that is becoming increasingly important in the current environment for most professional services:

4   *Competitive positioning messages*   these are directed as positioning the PSF in the mind of the target audience *vis-à-vis* existing or potential competitors, often on the basis of experience, quality, fees, etc. One of the best examples of this that I have seen was an advertisement by a small law firm specializing in conveyancing whose copy line read 'solicitors by name not by nature' in which they successfully positioned themselves against the negative perceptions often held by consumers of the legal profession.

Message selection

From the alternative messages generated the marketer will obviously choose the message which is most likely to achieve the desired outcome in the minds of the target audience. Twedt[5] has suggested that alternative potential messages should be evaluated on the bases of desirability (of the message, promise, image, information, etc. to the individuals/organizations in the target audience); exclusivity (is the audience likely to be receiving similar messages from competitors, etc.); and believability (is the message credible to the audience, can we prove it?).

Copy creation

Armed with the type of message that is most likely to be successful in creating the desired outcomes in the minds of the target audience, the marketer can physically create the message in terms of advertising copy. This is essentially the 'how' of the message decision and involves thinking about the style of the advertisement (layout of the words and headlines, etc.) and the words used and the presentation in terms of graphics (colour, shape, pictures, typeface, etc.). In general terms the simpler the copy the easier it is for the target audience to receive the message.[6] Obviously larger advertisements and more colourful advertisements are more likely to reach the attention of the target audience.

Media decisions

While message selection and copy/design creation are the 'how' part of advertising in terms of encoding the message, the other side of the 'how' coin, how to physically get the message to the target audience, is represented by a set of media decisions. The planner of the advertising

campaign is obviously looking for the mix of media that is most like
be used by the target market and that will provide cost-effectively
reach and frequency necessary for the reception of the des
message.

Media categories

Marketers have a wide choice in terms of media categories:

1 Print

Newspapers Many professional service firms advertise in newspapers, particularly in local newspapers for those firms dealing
primarily with consumer clients within a given geographic market.
Corporate professional service firms often advertise in business
sections of national newspapers such as the *Financial Times*, *The Sunday
Times*, etc.

Magazines These are used less frequently in general, but more
frequently by business-to-business professional service firms such as
accountants, corporate lawyers, architects, civil engineers, etc.
Specialist magazines can provide highly targetted and therefore
efficient media.

Directories Most professions have directories, compiled by their
professional bodies, of member firms, etc. but there are also a large
number of commercial directories printed. These range from *Yellow
Pages* and *Thomsons* guides to *Crawfords City Directory*. There are also
commercial directories of individual professions such as *The legal 500*
for the legal profession.

2 Mail

Many professionals (including myself and most of the firms I work
with) have been promised much by direct mail as a media channel,
particularly by those trying to sell marketing database systems. While
direct mail does allow good audience selectivity (providing that you
can buy or create accurate mailing lists) some professions still place
restrictions upon the types of direct mail that member firms can send.
These restrictions, coupled with growing resistance in most target
audiences to 'Junk Mail', have led many professional service firms to
adopt a 'softly softly' approach to direct mail, particularly since the cost
per audience member is relatively high.

3 Signs

Every professional service firm I have ever visited or worked with have used signs as a part of their marketing strategy. Many of them, however, did not realize this fact and may still not consider their brass plate on the door to be advertising – but of course it is. Signs both inside the office of a firm, and outside the office (even the traditional gold block letters on the window) convey an information message and an image-forming message to those who see them. Other parts of the sign media channel include transit (sides of buses, taxis, etc.) and billboards.

4 Electronic media

These media are probably the least widely used by professional service firms, largely because of the total cost and poor audience selectivity. While some of the big accountancy firms celebrated the 1984 relaxation of professional regulations with TV advertising campaigns this experiment with television has not been widely repeated. However, continued technological developments mean that TV advertising may become feasible as cheaper and more highly targetted cable and satellite stations become available. It is also possible to advertise on TV information networks such as ORACLE and other electronic networks such as PRESTEL, and some stockbroking firms have taken advantage of this.

More selective and cost efficient for many professional service firms are local radio stations. Again these are mainly used by PSFs who primarily deal with individual consumer clients such as high street solicitors.

5 Special media

This is very much a 'catch-all' category of everything else that may potentially include many media channels such as advertising in concert programmes, on T-shirts, on file covers, pens, golf balls, umbrellas, etc. Many of these media of the 'gift' type are used by professional service firms of all kinds.

The selection of the most appropriate and cost-effective media channel for the delivery of your campaign message will obviously be based upon a number of criteria which are likely to include:

- media habits of target audience;
- total cost of media;

- selectivity of media in reaching desired targets;
- type of message to be sent;
- media potential for demonstration, dramatization, visualization, etc.

Specific vehicles

In most cases, however, campaign planners rarely distinguish between media categories and the specific media vehicles available within each category, many of which overlap. The major specific media vehicles utilized by professional service firms are:

Print display advertisements, classified advertisements, inserts.
Mail letters, brochures, newsletters/bulletins, greeting cards, etc.
Electronic commercials, sponsorship.
Signs posters, plaques, etc.
Special media display advertisements.

Media timing

The timing decision with media may not simply be a choice that is made once media channels and specific vehicles have been fixed. Each of the media channels and vehicles will have different lead times and availability of slots, etc. For example, it takes a shorter period of time to plan and execute a display advertising campaign in several newspapers than to plan and distribute a brochure via direct mail. Similarly, a classified advertisement can be placed in a newspaper quicker than a poster campaign on the tube. If the timing of your message is important, e.g. the end of the tax year, budget day, etc. then unless campaigns are planned and ready to execute several months in advance, media choices open to the marketer will be limited.

Other timing decisions that need to be considered by campaign planners relate to the frequency of message delivery. This is a particularly difficult decision as there are obvious merits and demerits in each of the three main alternatives: burst advertising (a concentration of advertising messages in a short period of time, maybe frequent exposures to one advertisement or less frequent exposures to a number of different advertisements); continuous advertising (a lower frequency of exposures to the advertisement(s) sustained continuously throughout the year); and, intermittent advertising (small bursts of advertising activity at different times during a longer period).

Advertising evaluation

The final stage in the campaign management process concerns the evaluation of advertising. In theory the effectiveness of advertising campaigns may be enhanced by the pre-testing of copy, message and media upon a sample of the target audience. In reality few professional service firms consider themselves, or their advertising spend, sufficiently large to warrant experimental testing as a part of their campaign planning process. It is at this stage, however, that marketing research, which can be relatively cheap, can be conducted. This is particularly useful in uncovering the media habits of target audiences. Much more likely to be used in professional service firms are rudimentary measures of post-advertising response from target markets. These are most often conducted via so-called 'coupon response', i.e. the returning of tear-off requests for further information, etc. that may be included in direct mail literature and advertisements. Some degree of sophistication may be achievable with such analysis if it is possible to distinguish from which particular media vehicle the response was generated, and at what time, via some coding of the advertisements. This has the advantage of allowing the marketer to directly evaluate the response not only to the campaign but also to particular messages, formats, media and timing which will be useful in planning future campaigns.

In most cases, however, a more rudimentary evaluation of response to a campaign is likely to be made in terms of the number of written, telephone and personal enquiries made in the period during and following a campaign.

Unfortunately many professional service firms do not commit any time, effort or budget to evaluating post-campaign effectiveness let alone pre-testing. It is also true that in many of the firms that do engage in some rudimentary post-campaign response measurement this is often a way of justifying advertising budgets and budget requests rather than information which is included in the planning and execution of future campaigns.

While this chapter does provide a framework for dealing with the major decision areas in campaign planning, and does force marketers to make explicit choices between alternatives, many professional service firms still make mistakes with their advertising, running ill-covered and ineffective campaigns. This is even true in the USA in spite of the wider choice of media (particularly television and radio) and the greater time that American PSFs have been allowed to advertise.

In the accountancy profession in the USA Irwin Braun[7] identified seven major mistakes that are commonly made with campaigns:

1 Failing to target the advertising sufficiently to the needs of a particular audience.
2 Inability to position effectively *vis-à-vis* competition in advertisements and thereby achieve differentiation in the audience's mind.
3 Running advertisements too infrequently to achieve the desired objectives.
4 Information overload in advertisements – too much information and too many themes and ideas at once.
5 Uninspiring, uninteresting and unremarkable presentation and graphical design of advertisements.
6 Overconcentration upon professional service firm features, factual statements and technical service offerings and no concentration upon client benefits.
7 Overreliance upon newspaper advertising.

This may offer some comfort to professionals – at least they may not be alone in being largely unprofessional in their advertising activities – but is this really much comfort? The use of even a rudimentary campaign planning approach such as the one included in this chapter can minimize the risk of UK professionals repeating the mistakes made in the USA accountancy profession.

Advertising is still not considered a normal business activity for many professions and individual professional service firms. Even where advertising has been allowed for some time such as the USA and Canada there is still no uniform support for advertising amongst professionals.[8] From the perspective of the other side of the advertising coin – the target audience – there is some limited evidence from individual consumer client markets for legal services and physician services that consumers find advertising useful in terms of its information content in making choices between competing suppliers of these services.[9]

While many of the problems concerning the advertising of professional services are related to a lack of campaign planning along the lines suggested, there are some more general guidelines provided by George and Berry for the advertising of services, which are applicable to the professional services context.[10] These guidelines include:

Advertising to employees given the 'people intensive' nature of professional services, marketers need to be aware of the potential impact of campaigns upon employees and partners, and even to treat them as target audiences (this will be discussed in more detail in the final part of the book).
Capitalizing on word-of-mouth given the uncertainty associated with most professional services, potential clients often rely upon word-of-

mouth recommendations in making choices. Marketers therefore need to gear campaigns to maximize word-of-mouth recommendation by targetting referral sources, opinion leaders, etc. and perhaps even featuring client comments in advertisements.

Providing tangible clues tangibles are generally easier to evaluate than intangibles and consumers and individual decision makers are often more comfortable with the tangible. Advertisements may therefore be more effective if they emphasize tangible representations of the service offering, e.g. focus on the person of the professional or create a logo that signifies something tangible.

Making the service understood end users of many professional services do not fully understand the nature and content of the services that they may need, and advertisements may be useful to them in providing information which helps them to understand and therefore feel more certain in choosing professional services and providers.

Promising what is possible there is no quicker way to attract a client than to promise the earth and no faster way of losing a client than failing to deliver it. As we will see in the following section, overpromising is always a temptation when creating campaigns. However, while this may gain short-term advantage the long-run damage can be considerable.

References

1 Morgan, N. A. (1990), 'Communications and the reality of marketing in professional service firms', *International Journal of Advertising*, vol. 9, pp. 283–293.

2 Bloom, P. N. (1977), 'Advertising in the professions: the critical issues', *Journal of Marketing*, July, pp. 103–110; Stafford, D. C. (1988), 'Advertising in the professions: a review of the literature', *International Journal of Advertising*, vol. 7, pp. 189–200.

3 Schramm, W. (1971), 'How communications works', in Schramm, W. and Roberts, D. F. (eds), *The Process and Effects of Mass Communication'*, Urbana, Ill: University of Illinois Press.

4 Kotler, P. and Bloom, P. N. (1984), *Marketing Professional Services*, Englewood Cliffs, NJ: Prentice-Hall.

5 Twedt, D. W. (1969), 'How to plan new products, improve old ones, and create better advertising', *Journal of Marketing*, Jan, pp. 53–57.

6 Smith, B. E. (1980), 'Reaching the public: the CPA's new image', *Journal of Accountancy* (US), Jan, pp. 47–52.

7 Braun, I. (1982), 'Seven major mistakes accountants make in advertising', *The CPA Journal*, July, pp. 82–83.

8 Shimp, T. A. and Dyer, R. F. (1981), 'Factors influencing lawyers' satisfaction with advertising and intentions to continue advertising', in Donnelly J. H. and George W. R. (eds), *Marketing of Services*, Chicago, Ill:

AMA; Crane, F. G., Meacher, C. and Clarke, T. K. (1989), 'Lawyers' attitudes towards legal services advertising in Canada', *International Journal of Advertising*, vol. 8, pp. 71–78.

9   Hughes, M. A. and Kasulis, J. J. (1985), 'The production cue hypothesis and the marketing of legal services', in *Proceedings of American Institute for Decision Services Conference*, pp. 112–116; Johns, H. E. and Moser, H. R. (1989), 'An empirical analysis of consumers' attitudes towards physician advertising', *International Journal of Advertising*, vol. 8, pp. 35–45.

10 George, W.R. and Berry, L.L. (1981), 'Guidelines for the advertising of services', *Business Horizons*, July/August.

10 Marketing communications: personal selling and firm image

Of the major categories of promotional tools available to marketers and professionals, personal selling may be viewed as the most important. Personal selling will normally play a greater role in persuading prospective clients to become actual clients than advertising and public relations. In comparison to the other marketing communications tools available to professional service firms, personal selling offers flexibility in terms of message, the ability to 'customize' the service offering, two-way communications, opportunities to build confidence and almost complete control over the marketing message given to the prospective client. However, personal selling is also the most expensive marketing communications tool and offers the lowest reach of any of the available promotional media.

Within the professions personal selling suffers from something of an image problem to an even greater degree than marketing (amongst those that are sophisticated enough to distinguish between them). The popular typology of selling amongst professionals is that it is an undignified activity consisting of applying techniques of persuasion to innocent people that is undertaken by aggressive, overbearing, 'wide-boy' individuals who wear garish suits, and who can often earn a lot of money through commission. The reality of personal selling is that in the professional service context it is a meeting between professional(s) and the prospective client designed to facilitate a mutually satisfying exchange resulting in an instruction from the client. Not only is this reality a long way removed from the perceived mythology of selling but, in the case of many professional services, personal selling situations are invaluable sources of information that are used by prospective clients to choose between alternative professional service providers, or to ensure that purchase intentions to choose one firm are well founded.

One of the reasons that many professionals dislike selling even more than marketing is that selling as a responsibility is less easy to abdicate and pass on to somebody else. The buying behaviour of both individual consumers and organizations dictates that effective personal selling in the professional service context can only be undertaken by professionals themselves. Thus while we may view the evolution of marketing within professional service firms as a series of abdications of responsibility, this has been more difficult for professionals to achieve in the field of personal selling. Professionals do still, however, have largely negative views of personal selling and the bitter comment of 'I didn't become a professional to sell' has widespread applicability for a large number of professionals in every profession.

On the question of 'who should sell professional services?' the literature is in unusually widespread agreement. Few professional service firms have ever tried to organize a separate sales function with staff who concentrate simply upon selling the services of the firm. The buying situation, especially in new task buying, which is the focus of most explicit personal selling activity, is characterized by prospective client uncertainty. In such situations the prospective client is concerned with a number of service and problem-specific issues, but underlying all of this is the client's desire for confidence that the firm can provide by solving his or her problem. Confidence in these situations is normally sought by prospective clients in the person of the professional who will be responsible for delivering the service. It is therefore essential that the personal selling situation is managed and undertaken by the professional(s) who will be delivering the service to the potential client.

This view of personal selling in the professional service context has been proposed and supported by a number of the leading authors in the field.[1] Wittreich states that 'A professional service can only be purchased meaningfully from someone who is capable of rendering the service. Selling ability and personality by themselves are meaningless.'[2]

In spite of the widespread support for the notion that effective selling of professional services can only be undertaken by professionals, many professionals still attempt to abdicate responsibility for personal selling on the basis that they are not 'cut out' for selling. There appears to be a widespread belief that good salesmen are born not made. This has resulted in the old axiom of professionals being either 'finders, minders or grinders' being allowed to become an accepted and acceptable reality in most professional service firms. In any market-oriented firm all of the firm's professional staff need to be able to sell the services that they, and the firm, produces. This means that most professional service firms will need to attempt this through both recruitment and selection and training.

There have been numerous attempts to produce conclusive research results concerning the personality traits of effective sales people in manufacturing and marketing organizations. While the results of these research efforts have failed to develop conclusive evidence of specific personality traits in effective sales, a widely reported study by Mayer and Greenberg[3] identified two factors. Empathy (the ability to feel what the prospective purchaser feels) and ego drive (a strong personal desire/need to achieve success in the selling situation) were found to be predictors of sales force performance. However, little research to date has focused upon personal selling in the services sector in general, and the professional service sector in particular. In terms of guiding recruitment and selection decisions professionals may be better guided by the personality traits of the most effective personal sellers in their own organization.

The reality of the labour market, and the desirability of professionals who are effective personal sellers, will almost inevitably mean that it is impossible to fill all professional positions in a firm with individuals who exhibit empathy, ego drive or other situation-specific traits. Whatever the personality traits of the professionals within a firm, the ability of each individual in terms of effectiveness in personal selling activities can be enhanced through training and there are many organizations who offer such basic sales training in the UK and all over the world.

The personal selling process

The process of personal selling of professional services may be seen as a series of sequential steps (Figure 10.1). Planning the personal selling activities of the professionals in a firm may be enhanced by a recognition of the various stages involved in successfully selling a professional service-offering to a prospective client.

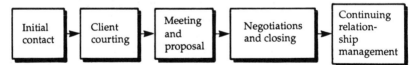

Figure 10.1 *The personal selling process*

Initial contact

The initial contact between a professional service firm and a prospective client is obviously the starting point of the selling process. This is also the part of the process that many professionals find most difficult. The words 'cold calling' are enough to strike terror in the hearts of many commercial sales representatives let alone professionals. This is probably the one part of the selling process that is most objectionable to professionals. For any planned programme of personal selling to be successfully implemented it has first to overcome the problem of cold calling and professionals' fear and loathing of it. There are two extreme approaches to this: the first is brute force. I have seen two partners in a provincial law firm bullied into making five 'cold calls' each via a telephone in the boardroom with scripts and pressure supplied by a marketing consultant. This not only had the effect of driving the two partners into an uncomfortable position but also managed to reinforce every prejudice that most of the professionals in that firm felt against selling in particular and marketing in general.

The other extreme is to do no 'cold calling' at all and to rely upon contact being made unprompted by prospective clients and using these qualified leads as the basis for personal selling programmes. This is far more palatable to the average professional but is likely to lead to less new clients. Again, the most effective approach to this stage of the selling process probably lies somewhere between these extremes for most professional service firms.

In an 'ideal' world all client leads would come from clients knocking on our door saying 'I've got a problem, can you help me please?' In reality this does not happen often enough to satisfy most PSFs' desire for new clients. Hopefully, however, while our other marketing communications activities may not have engendered an uncontrollable desire to batter down our door with requests for help by our target market, marketing communications programmes should have left a percentage of our target market with a recognition of our name and probably a smaller percentage with a bit more knowledge such as the type of work we do, specialisms, location, etc. Cold calling is a lot easier to 'sell' to professionals if calls are answered by contacts whose initial reaction is 'Oh you're the firm on Market Street who specialize in . . .' than 'Who? . . . I've never heard of you . . .'

Most professionals are amenable to some form of what I have come to call 'warm calling' – bringing together professionals and members of a target market in a non 'hard sell' environment. One of the best ways of achieving this is via a seminar or workshop on a topic important to the target market that is within the firm's capabilities, expertise and service offering. Less direct methods of achieving the same ends – initial contact with a prospective client (a qualified lead in the sales jargon) are through topical publications direct mailed to target audiences, coupon requests for further information with advertisements, corporate hospitality events and membership of clubs, societies, etc.

To a large extent all of these approaches are more successful than either of the two extremes in the professional service context since they are usually more acceptable to professionals and are therefore more likely to be actively implemented by them. They also provide more 'qualified' leads on prospective clients since the audiences are to a much greater extent self-selected and are more likely to comprise of those who recognize the need for a professional service of some kind. In deciding upon audiences for such events and activities professional service firms need to remember the importance of referral sources in most professional service markets and include them as key members of target audiences.

Client courting

At this stage of the selling process the professional is actively following up the initial contact and attempting to sustain the interest of the prospective client and build confidence in the professional service firm. Wittreich[4] identifies two approaches to client courting: the extrinsic, which primarily involves informing the prospective client of the personnel, abilities, experience and success stories of the firm; and the intrinsic, which involves focusing upon the client's problem, grasping the problem to a degree which is sufficient to build client confidence and building upon the problem diagnosis through questioning, information-seeking and preliminary reports on the problem directed back to the client.

While Wittreich argues that the intrinsic approach is preferred there are likely to be elements of both approaches in effective personal selling. However, an approach that is dominated by listening, questioning and information collection during the courtship phase is more likely to be successful than approaches dominated by telling and informing. Focusing upon understanding the specifics of a prospective client's problem is the basis of effective personal selling in the short term as well as of effective marketing in the longer term.

It is essential that at this stage the prospective client is introduced to the key professional personnel who will be involved in solving that prospect's problem should the instructions be given. Prospective clients' confidence, the critical underlying element in the selling situation, is more likely to be gained by, and given to, individual professionals, than by the entity of a firm.

Meeting and proposal

If the courtship is successful then in the purchase of most professional services (particularly by organizational clients) there will be a meeting between prospective client and professional in which a written or verbal proposal will be put before the prospective client for consideration and as a basis on which to proceed to undertaking professional service work. If the initial contact was an invitation to attend a beauty parade, submit a proposal or tender for a project, then this stage of the selling process is likely to include a formal presentation.

In general, proposals are more likely to be well received by clients if they:

- Are built around an in-depth analysis of the problem/situation facing the client and therefore focus upon client needs.
- Focus more on the benefits to the client of the approach/service offering suggested in the proposal, than upon technical minutiae of the proposed solution.
- Are written in a language that is easily understood by the prospective client.
- Highlight how the approach taken, solution offered, etc. is likely to differ from those offered by competing professional service suppliers.

It also helps if the proposal looks like a serious analysis prepared for an individual prospective client based upon the specific situation or problems that they face. Many professional service firms, of all kinds, attempt to routinize their proposals as much as possible. In terms of providing models of 'best' approaches to proposal preparation this is a useful guide for professionals. However, on a number of occasions I have seen beautifully word-processed, laser-printed, Leatherette-bound proposals that halfway through revert to the name of the professional service firm's last prospective client. Needless to say this does not engender a feeling of confidence, client closeness and understanding between the prospective client and the firm.

Client negotiation and closing

In order to reach this stage of the selling process the professional has to have convinced the prospective client that:

1 A problem situation/client need exists.
2 It is in the client's interest to solve the problem/satisfy the need.
3 The problem/need has been correctly identified and diagnosed.
4 The solution/service offered by the professional is appropriate.

5 The professional/firm is capable of providing the proposed solution/service.

These points need to be established and re-established by the professional(s) in the prospective client's mind. The basis of additional information, once these points have been established, is the acceptability to the client of the timing of the proposed solution/service offering, the professional staff who will deliver the solution/service and manage the client/service interface, and the proposed fee level and fee schedule.

Two important elements in any negotiation between professional and prospective client at this stage of the selling process are objections and trial closing.

In most negotiations professionals will encounter some implicit or explicit objections to the proposal, staff, fee or timing. It is important that professionals are trained, or at least made aware of potential objections and techniques for overcoming them. Listman[5] suggests that professionals can handle client objections during the negotiation phase of the selling process in at least seven different ways.

1 Explain (agree to the objection then qualify the agreement).
2 Reverse (turn the objection into another selling point).
3 Admit (agree that the objection is valid and modify the proposal).
4 Delay (delay answering the objection).
5 Ignore (in some situations clients may say things they don't believe).
6 Deny (show the objection to be invalid).
7 Qualify (ask for a further explanation of the objection).

Professionals cannot be allowed to view objections as personal insults, unwanted confrontations or obstacles to be avoided.

For a successful conclusion to the personal selling process it is important that professionals realize that potential clients' objections are best dealt with by making them explicit and dealing with them, rather than trying to avoid them and move as quickly as possible to 'closing' the sale.

Most professionals view the 'closing' part of the negotiation process as similarly difficult and even something they find difficult to confront. Almost every professional will fear the prospective client saying 'no' at this stage as this may result in feelings of failure, personal rejection and damage to any further relationship with the prospective client. Again, most professionals can gain a great deal from training in negotiation and closing.

Any training in this area needs to get professionals to understand

and practise 'trial closing'. Trial closing is the building up of a series of acceptances, degrees of agreement and determination of a client's readiness to 'close' the negotiation. A series of 'trial closes' should be used before the professional ultimately closes by asking explicitly for the engagement, appointment, contract, etc. Trial closing does often involve techniques such as gaining prospective client agreement with component parts of the proposal such as the problem definition and the proposed solution, summarizing the key selling points, moving past the close with discussions concerning what might happen after the close 'assuming we take on this assignment we would then . . .', etc. Such trial closing techniques used throughout the negotiation will help the professional to feel more confident about closing the sale at the appropriate moment.

Client management

The basis of the prosperity, growth or even survival of most professional service firms is dependent not upon obtaining new clients, but upon retaining existing clients. It is therefore essential that once a professional has successfully completed the preceding stages of the personal selling process, the client/firm relationship is managed in order to maximize the likelihood of retaining the client. Market research that I have undertaken in the corporate legal services sector demonstrates that clients interface with individuals in professional service firms not with the firms themselves. Clients prefer firms in which they have a long-term relationship with a named and known individual within the firm. One of the key causes of client dissatisfaction is the changing of the individuals within the firm responsible for interfacing with them and managing the relationship. The relationship manager for each key client should be the focus for all communication and information between the firm and the client.

Firm image: corporate identity and public relations

The issue of firm or 'corporate' image is dominant in most professionals' thinking about non-personal marketing communications. The importance of firm/corporate image is also evident in the services marketing literature where the difficulty of using branding (which dominates non-personal marketing communications in many manufacturing sectors) in the service context has led some academics to consider corporate image as an alternative communications approach.[6] While within the professions corporate image seems to

169

mean a number of different things to different professionals (often based upon which particular type of marketing communications firms the professionals have been approached by in the past!) it is essentially a relatively simple communications concept. Corporate or firm image is the perception of the reality of the firm held in the minds of its clients, competitors, potential marketplace and other relevant 'publics'.

Most professional service firms will never have undertaken a planned corporate identity programme that consisted of decisions other than which colour the firm should use for its headed notepaper. This does not, however, mean that most firms do not have a corporate identity. Every firm will have its own relevant publics who will hold perceived images of the firm, its professional and non-professional staff, its service offerings, etc. based upon past and present interaction with the firm, its clients, referral sources and information from the various media. There are, however, an increasing number of large professional service firms, in every profession, that have undertaken formalized corporate identity programmes with specialist advisors and often large budgets.

Corporate image is an important variable in the communications planning of service firms of all kinds for a number of very good reasons. First, a well-conceived and successfully implemented corporate identity programme can increase the likelihood of potential clients gaining and retaining name awareness – the first stage in the professional service firm selection stage of the purchase decision process. Thus a corporate identity programme, as a part of an integrated marketing communications effort, can increase the chances of a professional service firm being asked to take part in a beauty parade, make a presentation or give a proposal to a potential client.

Corporate image is also a concept that is inextricably interwoven with the idea of positioning. Positioning in the professional service context is essentially the planned development of an image of the firm in the minds of the relevant publics which differentiates it upon one or more bases from competitors. This is a particularly important concept for professional service firms to grasp and operationalize given the propensity of consumers and organizations to fail to differentiate between providers of 'generic' professional service offerings.[7] The results of a recent study of positioning in the insurance market provide a useful framework for professionals to begin to think about the positioning of the major firms in their marketplace and how their own position relates to both competitors and client needs.[8] Eight dimensions of service positioning were identified:

1 The reputation of the organization in terms of expertise, reliability, innovativeness and performance.
2 Augmentation of the 'product' offering i.e. 'product' augmentation, 'extra' service.
3 'People' advantage.
4 Superior 'packaging'.
5 Superior 'product' through technology.
6 Accessibility.
7 Customization.
8 More complete 'product' range.

Each of these dimensions offers possible bases for establishing a planned position in the minds of the 'public' of a professional service firm.

Many professionals think of corporate image, corporate identity, service positioning, etc. as essentially creative exercises, and they are encouraged in this belief by public relations consultants, design and graphics professionals and advertising agencies. There is, however, a problem with this belief, namely that existing clients (the key to any professional service firm's growth and profitability as discussed in Chapters 1 and 2) and many potential clients create their own image of the firm based upon past and present interaction and word-of-mouth information. Thus to a large degree the corporate image and positioning of a professional service firm for its most important target 'public' is based upon the reality of personal experience of the firm as perceived by clients and referral sources. While it may be possible in the short run to create an identity and position for a professional service firm in the minds of many 'publics' that is not based in the reality of the firm, its personnel, experiences and service offerings, the power of personal experience and word-of-mouth communication will ensure that such an image is not sustainable.[9]

Thus in considering the issue of corporate image in the professional service context, professionals need to remember two key points. First, that however well planned and executed a corporate image exercise, the image of the firm held by potential clients is not sufficient to motivate them to engage the firm. Second, that images created need to have some basis in the reality of the firm, its staff and service offerings if they are to be sustainable past the very short term. You can fool some of the people in your target markets for a very short time but you will never be given the opportunity to do business with them again.

Developing a corporate image programme

As with most marketing and strategic management decisions corporate image programmes can be viewed as a sequential series of decisions leading to a corporate image plan.

1 Image assessment

As with all forms of planning in marketing it is a little difficult to formulate a plan without concrete knowledge of where you are starting from. This is an area in which market research can provide useful, insightful, often inexpensive, and frequently surprising, information. Relatively simple market research can be undertaken with a sample of each of the firm's most relevant 'publics', i.e. groups of individuals and organizations who have an interest in, and/or potential impact upon, the firm and its performance. In terms of image assessment the most important publics to be researched are likely to be: employees, existing clients, past clients, potential clients in target markets, referral sources and possibly the media.

The results of image assessment research are often presented in a form known as multi-dimensional scaling which is a marketer's way of saying a grid with two different axes. This approach is also useful when the image assessment stage of the corporate image development process includes positioning information such as comparative image assessment of competing firms from the same publics (see Figure 10.2).

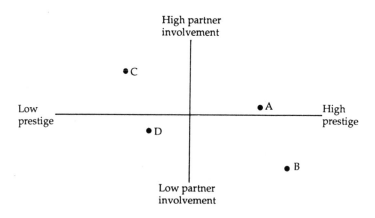

Figure 10.2 *Image assessment and positioning information*

In working with a medium-sized engineering consultancy partnership on developing a positioning statement as a basis for a corporate image programme two dimensions were found to be important to buyers in selecting consulting engineering firms for private hospital building work: the perceived prestige of the firm (on the basis that this somewhat reduced the risk in purchasing engineering services); and the degree of direct partner involvement in the day-to-day management of projects. The research and multi-dimensional scaling produced for firm 'A' revealed that against their major competitors for work in this area there was a potentially effective image and positioning statement as the prestige firm that had the highest partner involvement in projects. This is a potentially powerful competitive move since the programme is attempting to communicate how the firm is different from its major competitors upon bases that are recognized and valued by existing and potential clients.

As with all forms of market research, unless your firm has an in-house unit or someone trained in market research techniques, get an outside agency to undertake the research work to ensure credible and objective findings. One of the 'surprising' parts of this type of image assessment research is that it frequently reveals that there is a gap between the image of the firm held by its partners and employees, and the image held by existing and potential clients, and even referral sources. The existence of such 'perceptual' gaps is often difficult for partners and managers to face and it is therefore important that the research is as credible as possible. As discussed in Chapter 4 with relation to market analysis the human reaction to challenging, surprising or even unwelcome research information is to question the validity of the research techniques and competence of the researchers themselves.

2   Desired image plan

Armed with the knowledge of how a firm is currently perceived by its relevant publics the marketer needs to return at this point to the strategic marketing plan. If the strategic marketing plan contains even only the most rudimentary elements of market segmentation and competitive differentiation, then the marketer will have some guidelines as to the 'desired image' that the firm wishes to create in the minds of its most important publics.

It has to be remembered that it is important that a corporate image programme is related to the strategies devised in the strategic marketing planning process. Simply because corporate image may be seen as a tactical rather than strategic issue does not mean that the two are unrelated. Corporate image programmes may best be viewed as part of the operationalization and implementation of a strategic marketing plan. In any corporate image programme the desired image plan will be an amalgamation of what, ideally, the corporate image needs to be in order to achieve the objectives of the strategic marketing plan and, having researched the current image assessment, what it is possible and necessary to do to achieve this desired image.

There are a number of tools and media available for achieving the objectives set in the desired image plan. In any formalized corporate image programme it is likely that all of these will be used in order to ensure that the desired image is received and retained by the firm's most relevant publics. These major tools and media are:

3 Media relations

It is in the area of media relations, i.e. interfacing between the firm and the relevant media (newspapers, journals, magazines, TV, radio, etc.) that inform its publics, that the foundations and major expertise of PR people are to be found (indeed for many years PR was often interpreted as standing for press relations rather than public relations). There are always media that are interested in carrying stories that may be deemed to be 'newsworthy' in some respect, and it is up to the firm to ensure that the amount and type of exposure it receives in the media is sufficient to meet its corporate image needs. Preparing press releases and communicating effectively with the media are the areas in which firms benefit most from PR consultancy help.

Many firms, however, still expend too much effort in interfacing with the journals and magazines that relate to their profession and are read largely by other professionals, and not enough time and effort interfacing with media that are important to existing and potential clients.

Media relations, if handled carefully, can provide very credible exposure in the eyes of potential and existing clients since the media itself carries unsponsored and therefore more objective messages to the firm's publics. Thus an article in the *Financial Times* which describes a law firm as widely recognized as having specialist expertise in the area of city fraud and 'insider trading', carrying a quote from a partner in this firm's specialist department as a part of a news report on a particular event, sends a more powerful, memorable and 'objective' message to readers than a full-page colour advertisement in the same issue of the same newspaper. This obviously means that it is the media employees who have control over the message carried and not the firm and this is obviously a disadvantage *vis-à-vis* media advertising. However, the objectivity of the media does confer much more credibly on the message. If a firm is serious about managing its media relations then it has to recognize that it is a long-term process of relationship-building with a number of writers, reporters, researchers, editors, etc. in a number of different media, and that building such relationships takes time and effort on the part of the professional.

Most professional service firms, even those with expensive public relations help, largely ignore the potential benefits of actually writing articles for magazines and journals. To a certain extent this type of media relations provides the best combination of advertising and PR since it is not 'paid for' sponsorship and therefore has some degree of objectivity conferred upon it by being published, and it offers the firm greater control over the message. A particularly useful way of coming to the attention of potential clients is writing articles upon subjects of interest, in which the firm has some expertise, and publishing them in media used by potential clients (and existing clients) in target markets. This has produced very good contacts and results for management consultancy firms, accountancy and law firms and even consulting engineering and architectural practices. Most firms still, however, either ignore this aspect of media relations or fail to take it seriously enough.

4 Brochures

The planning, design, production and circulation of brochures still dominates the role of marketing communications (and even the role of marketing itself) in many professionals' minds. Given the antagonism, arguments, in-fighting and ill-feeling that often accompany brochure design and the mediocrity of most professional service firms' resulting brochures, it is possible to suggest that firms should forget brochures altogether as a promotional tool.

Potential clients do, however, have a need for information upon which to make comparisons and decisions and in many marketplaces brochures are specifically asked for. Thus it may well be that brochures are becoming a necessity in many professional service marketplaces simply because potential clients ask for them and competing firms produce them. If this is the case, then it is up to the professionals to ensure that the design and production of a brochure is kept in some sort of perspective by following a few commonsense guidelines:

- Do not try to design a brochure yourself – get professional help, preferably from a graphic design agency.
- Do not attempt to write the copy yourself – this usually results in disastrous brochures (it's even worse to get different sections written by different people – it shows!).
- Do not attempt to get everything you possibly can into one brochure for the whole firm. This can lead to confusing, complicated messages that are difficult to understand.
- Brochures about specific services or types of service are usually more valuable than brochures about the entire firm. A range of

brochures with one short brochure about the firm itself and a number of specialist brochures about specific service offerings is the optimal position.

- Attempt to make brochures look and 'feel' different to those of your major competitors.
- Use pictures, photographs, graphics and copy that create tangible representations of the service offerings and the firm, e.g. photographs of key personnel, descriptions of work undertaken for other clients, etc.

Also in the same category as brochures are newsletters which are used as written communications media to existing and potential clients in target markets by a number of large professional service firms. These are largely a tool for maintaining name awareness and interest amongst potential clients by demonstrating what the firm's professionals know and actually do in areas that might be of interest to the client. As with brochures, these can be expensive and time-consuming to prepare in-house and are most effective in their marketing communications role if they are focused towards individual target market segments. This, however, will obviously increase the production costs. In smaller professional service firms the cost in terms of partner and professional time can outweigh both the marketing production costs and the potential benefits.

5   House style

House style is a term much used by 'creative' types such as PR consultants and graphic design agencies. It essentially refers to a standardized format to be used throughout the firm in all its communications in terms of logo, headed paper, colours, sizes, etc. Potentially, the most important component of this is the logo (graphical representation of the firm's name or symbol). While a 'professional' image necessitates the use of a graphic designer for the development of a logo in even smaller professional service firms, the benefits of spending tens or even hundreds of thousands of pounds on a corporate identity programme seem to be relatively limited. In every profession there are a number of dominant firms who possess what are widely acknowledged to be poor logos, etc. and yet enjoy good images in the minds of relevant publics and have highly-regarded professional reputations. Thus the major guideline for house styles would seem to be to get professional help in terms of logo design (but this need not be terribly expensive) and make sure that the firm uses the same logos, colours, notepaper, invoices, etc. to ensure consistency.

6 Seminars/workshops

The final media/tool for image development is the use of seminars and workshops. These can provide relatively inexpensive ways of helping existing clients and therefore increasing the probability of long-term relationships and repeat business. They can also be aimed at particular target markets in order to introduce the firm to potential clients. This is a particularly useful communications tool since it brings professionals and potential/existing clients together in a face-to-face situation (which is necessary in the purchase decision process of most professional services).

Workshop/seminars run individually by a firm are usually best received if they are made as specific as possible to the needs of a particular target group and if they are free or very cheap. They will also need to include some 'mingling' time in order to allow delegates and staff to get together and chat more informally.

It is also possible to speak at events organized by professional conference organizations or outside bodies. This can be a cheap way into this form of marketing communications for smaller firms but obviously provides fewer personal selling opportunities and less control over the arrangements and content of the event. It is obviously necessary for firms who wish to pursue this route to identify conference organizations and potentially interested outside parties, and to contact them with details of individuals, professionals, qualifications, experience, speciality and availability.

Organizing and running your own seminars, etc. can be time-consuming and relatively expensive (dependent upon location, etc.). It may be useful to rely upon conference organizers (either independent organizers or those employed by specific venues) or even public relations people to aid the organization and running of a conference. In-house seminars using the firm's facilities can be relatively cheap and are often a useful way of running workshops/seminars aimed at retaining existing clients and encouraging cross-selling of services.

While these types of events are an effective tool in an integrated marketing communications programme, particularly in the latter stages of a specific campaign since they identify those potential clients in a target market who are interested enough to attend, and provide a vehicle and setting for moving 'interested' potential clients into active clients, via face-to-face communication and personal selling, seminars also have a nasty habit of going wrong, looking amateurish and creating a poor impression if they are not very carefully planned. Be careful!

A word of warning

While there is a legitimate and fruitful role for public relations consultants in the marketing communications programmes and activities of professional service firms the usefulness and field of expertise of PR consultants should not be overestimated. PR people are often the first representatives of marketing communications to come into contact with professional service firms, who are looking for help with their marketing development. Unfortunately, in my experience, and the experience of many professional service firms, many PR consultants use this initial contact, and most professionals' ignorance of marketing, to 'sell' entire communications programmes to firms, often for extortionate retainers and fees.

Professionals need to be aware that PR consultants are expert in, and of primary use to, professional service firms in terms of media relations. PR consultants are certainly *not* marketing strategists, marketing researchers or even advertising campaign planners or brochure designers. Beware of PR consultants who claim they can do all of this. I have seen too many inadequate so-called 'marketing plans' prepared by such PR consultants, and too many misleading and subjective 'research' reports along with badly designed brochures, to believe the claims of many PR consultants to be 'marketers'.

'Professional' PR consultants will tell you that they cannot even begin to perform their marketing communications role for a professional service firm until a detailed strategic marketing plan has been prepared by an experienced marketing planner (preferably via partner planning teams) with access to objective market analysis and research. This is not the job of the public relations consultant, and is beyond the competence and capability of the vast majority of them.

References

1 Wittreich, W. J. (1966), 'How to buy/sell professional services', *Harvard Business Review*, March–April, pp. 127–138; Gummesson, E. (1979), 'The marketing of professional services – an organisational dilemma', *European Journal of Marketing*, vol. 13, no. 5; Denney, R. W. (1981), 'How to develop – and implement – a marketing plan for your firm', *Practical Accountant* (US), July.
2 Wittreich, W. J., op. cit., p. 128.
3 Mayer, D. and Greenberg, H. M. (1964), 'What makes a good salesman?', *Harvard Business Review*, July–August, pp. 119–125.
4 Wittreich, W. J., op. cit., pp. 128–9.
5 Listman, R. J. (1988), *Marketing Accounting Services*, Homewood, Illinois: Dow Jones-Irwin, p. 185.

6 Bessom, R. M. and Jackson, D. W. (1975), 'Service retailing: a strategic marketing approach', *Journal of Retailing*, Summer; Onkvisit, S. and Shaw, J. J. (1989), 'Service marketing: image, branding and competition', *Business Horizons*, Jan/Feb, pp. 13–18.

7 Bradlow, D. A. (1986), 'Positioning the professional service firm', *Legal Economics*, vol. 12, pp. 30–35.

8 Easingwood, C. and Mahajan, V. (1989), 'Positioning of financial services for competitive advantage', *Journal of Product and Innovation Management*, vol. 6, no. 1.

9 Gronroos, C. (1984), *Strategic Management and Marketing in the Service Sector*, London: Chartwell-Bratt; Normann, R. (1984), *Service Management: Strategy and Leadership in Service Businesses*, Chichester: John Wiley.

Part Five
Making Marketing Happen

One of the fundamental problems that exists with marketing in most sectors, and in professional service firms more than most, is that it is relatively easy to acquire the trappings of marketing but very difficult to instil the substance. At its present stage of development within the professions, marketing is still very much at the 'trappings' end of the spectrum.

The trappings of marketing in the professional service context may be seen as the glossy brochures, the PR consultants, the new corporate identity, the advertising campaign and, in some cases, even the marketing manager or marketing assistant. The cost associated with all of these items may well be tens or even hundreds of thousands of pounds and will represent a sizable marketing budget for most PSFs.

Alone, the trappings of marketing are unlikely to have a significant impact upon the amount of business a PSF does or, more importantly, the way in which it does it. The substance of marketing may be seen as the implementation of the marketing concept; that is developing a market orientation that is recognized, shared and constantly worked at by all the members of the firm. The financial cost of achieving this 'substance' of marketing is likely to be less than that of achieving the trappings mentioned above. However, achieving a market orientation and developing a client focus throughout the firm is likely to take a lot longer to implement than the trappings. Perhaps more importantly, achieving a market orientation calls for organization-wide changes in structure, culture, management philosophy and the way in which the firm interacts with the marketplace it serves.

The costs of developing a market-oriented firm are far more important in terms of professional and employee adaptation to the change involved rather than any financial costs that may be incurred. If marketing is to evolve beyond the trappings stage, however, and the goal of becoming market-led, to which so many firms and professionals pay lip-service, is to become achievable, then the issues of implementation and the management of change in the professional service context need to move to the top of the management agenda.

11 Developing a market orientation

It is clear that many partners, professionals and marketers believe that the primary objective of introducing marketing into the professional service context is the development of a market-oriented firm. While some firms may not recognize the term 'market oriented' they often substitute other titles such as 'client centred', 'market-led', 'market-driven', 'client focused', etc. In essence these amount to the same thing – the development of a market-oriented professional service firm as the overriding goal of the firm's organizational, marketing and strategic development. There appears to be emerging within the professions a widely held view that in the future a market orientation will be a prerequisite for competitive success, fee income and profitability in the increasingly deregulated and dynamic markets for professional services.

In spite of this widely held belief that a market orientation is becoming a competitive necessity in the professional service context it appears that there is relatively little unanimity about what a market orientation is, what it entails in professional service firms, and how best such an orientation may be achieved. To some degree this uncertainty has been reflected in the academic literature concerning market orientation over the past twenty-five years.

Early perspectives on the issue of market orientation focused upon the role of the marketing function and the structural issue of marketing activities and responsibilities. In essence this perspective related market orientation to marketing organization by viewing the implementation of the marketing concept as concerned with the creation of a marketing department, with a powerful chief marketing executive who had direct responsibility for a whole range of strategic and tactical marketing activities for the firm.[1]

A later perspective took the 'ing' out of marketing orientation and focused instead upon the cultural orientation of the organization. In this view the role and function of a marketing department was seen as the 'trappings' of a market orientation at best, and irrelevant at worst. The key issue in this perspective of a market orientation was the cultural characteristics of an organization in the way that a 'customer focus' was evidenced in the culture and activities of an organization. Thus in order to achieve a market orientation the critical goal was to create an organizational culture that exhibited a strong customer focus.[2]

These existing views of market orientation have recently been synthesized with empirical investigation in the USA as a part of the recent resurgence of interest in market orientation. A new view of the market-orientation construct has emerged which is receiving widespread support. This is probably best expressed in the work of Kohli and Jaworski (1990) who have offered a new formal definition of market orientation.

> Market orientation is the organizational generation of market intelligence pertaining to current and future customer needs, dissemination of the intelligence across departments, and organization-wide responsiveness to it.[3]

Why do we want to be market oriented?

While it is clear that many professionals across all professions believe that the development of a market orientation is a critical goal in the organizational development of professional service firms, it is rather less clear why this belief is so widely held and the reasoning that underlies it. It appears that, as with the introduction of marketing into the professions, the increasing focus upon the achievement of a market orientation is driven by increasingly competitive marketplaces rather than any altruistic notion of faith in the marketing concept. As with marketing, market orientation is a 'distress purchase' on the part of most professional service firms.

As a marketing academic it has always been an issue of concern that few robust empirical studies were able to prove a causal relationship between market orientation and organization performance. While many believe that this link does exist, it has proven particularly difficult to develop valid measures of market orientation and robust measurements of performance while controlling enough environmental variables to establish a satisfactory relationship. Thus marketers have been forced to cope with the difficulties of marketing a 'market orientation' perspective on professional service firm development with no robust evidence that this would impact upon the firm's bottom line.

Recent developments in the USA have, however, seen two independent studies establish relationships between market orientation and business performance across a wide number of commercial sectors.[4] While these studies have not been based in the professional services sector specifically, the results from business-to-business and consumer service businesses seem to be in line with other commercial sectors and the results may well be generalizable to all types of commercial organization.

The Kohli and Jaworski model[5] goes further and predicts three sets of consequences of a market orientation: (i) increased performance in indicators such as ROI, profitability, etc., (ii) employee responses in terms of better *esprit de corps*, greater job satisfaction, and higher commitment to the organization and (iii) customer responses in terms of customer satisfaction, customer loyalty, repeat business and customers' willingness to recommend. It would therefore seem that in spite of the historical absence of proof, the new focus upon the issue of market orientation has begun to explain and test the relationship between market orientation and a set of consequences that will be attractive to most professional service firms.

A market orientation

Before moving on to the question of 'how' to achieve a market orientation and thus enjoy the consequences, it is worth considering exactly what it is we are attempting to achieve, i.e. what are the critical components of a market orientation? In the new market orientation 'movement' within the academic world there is a surprising degree of congruence between the findings of the main researchers in this area. The critical components of market orientation may be synthesized as consisting of three main 'pillars'.

- Finding out, at a 'needs' level, what it is that customers/clients currently want and how these needs are likely to change in the future, and recognizing and predicting the role of existing and potential competitors in the dynamics of the marketplace.
- Getting everyone in the organization to understand the marketing concept and sharing with them all the information and research generated about the customers, competition and marketplace.
- Co-ordinating and encouraging inter-departmental, organization-wide activities to focus upon responding to the current and anticipated needs of the customers/clients.

These three points encompass the measures of market orientation proposed by Kohli and Jaworski and Narver and Slater, as well as receiving the widespread support of the existing literature covering this area.

The area of greatest concern, and greatest confusion, amongst professionals, partners, consultants and ultimately professional service firms, is how exactly a firm achieves a market orientation. The question that I am asked most often during meetings, seminars, workshops, etc. is 'What can my firm actually do in order to achieve a market orientation?' The first thing that all professionals have to realize is that there is no 'quick fix' approach to achieving a market orientation in a short space of time. If such a solution did exist everyone would apply it with a zero-sum gain in competitive terms and a loss in financial terms for all professional service firms.

While there are no 'quick fix' solutions there are a number of goals, some more readily achievable than others, that need to be attained in order to achieve a market orientation in the longer run.

Partner understanding and commitment

Any movement towards becoming a market-oriented firm has to begin by getting the partners within the firm to understand what a market orientation is, what it involves, and critically, why it is necessary. Given the current professional production orientation of the over-whelming majority of professional service firms, any movement towards a market orientation is likely to entail the firm, its partners and employees in:

Cultural change

While many professionals talk glibly about changing organizational cultures and many management consultants even claim to be able to bring about cultural change within organizations, the reality of organization culture makes this aspect of a market orientation difficult to analyse and manage.

While academics may argue about what exactly defines an organization's culture, a reasonable working definition will describe culture as a set of shared beliefs, values and norms amongst the members of an organization that describes 'the way we do things here'. While there is still a lot that business academics do not know about organizational culture, one thing that we do know is that culture is inextricably tied to the people within the organization and that the only way in which culture can be radically altered, in a relatively short space of time, is to change the people within the organization – that is literally by replacing them. This is not an option that is open to most firms outside the start-up situation. We therefore have to accept that culture change in professional service firms can only be achieved increment-ally because it involves changing the attitudes and beliefs of those within the organization.

Structural change

If a market orientation means organizing workflows, communications, and professionals and support staff in terms of configuring the professional service firm in such a way that it is best able to meet current and anticipated client needs, then this is likely to involve considerable structural change for most professional service firms. Simple organization, such as formal departmentalization based either upon service-offering type or client sector with centralized support functions, is unlikely to be the most effective configuration of the firm's resources in terms of meeting client needs. Since these types of organization dominate amongst firms in most professions, the achievement of a market orientation is likely to call for considerable structural change within most professional service firms.

Process change

An understanding, at a needs level, of what clients actually want from a professional service firm, and the criteria upon which they evaluate quality is also likely to impact upon how professional services are produced and delivered to clients. This type of process change, i.e. changes in the way in which professional services are produced, the context in which the service is produced and the location and interaction between firm and client in the delivery of the professional service, will obviously be connected with the structural changes outlined above.

Systems change

As a result of the above changes that are implicit in achieving a market orientation, professional service firms are also likely to need to change the formal and informal systems by which the firm is managed, run and controlled. A particularly important part of this systems change, as we shall see later, may be the formal reward system and the formal and informal recognition systems of the firm.

All of these changes are obviously interlinked, potentially very large scale, and probably together form the core of the barriers that need to be overcome in achieving a market-oriented professional service firm. The simple truth is that most people, both as individuals and collectively, are resistant to change. Generally speaking the greater the change the more people are resistant towards it. In terms of introducing a market orientation to most professional service firms the changes that will need to be made by all of the people within the firm are both fundamental and significant.

It is therefore vitally important that before even attempting to introduce a market orientation a significant degree of understanding and commitment is achieved amongst the partnership. In particular, partners will need to be aware of the type and magnitude of the changes that both they and the employees of the firm will have to make. The changes implicit in achieving a market-oriented firm may be considered as the real 'price' of becoming market oriented. This may well be one of the reasons that attempts to become market oriented in most professional service firms to date have focused upon acquiring the 'trappings' such as PR advisors, publications, corporate identity and even marketing managers/assistants. While these trappings may be expensive in terms of the budgets involved they do not necessitate the type and degree of change implicit in the 'substance' of a market orientation.

Partner signs and signals

Having obtained the understanding of market orientation, and all that it entails for a professional service firm, it is essential that partners demonstrate their commitment to the achievement of a market orientation by sending the appropriate signs and signals to the staff of the firm.

The notion of sending signs and signals for the consumption of the employees of a professional service firm is allied to the necessity for cultural change in order to achieve a market orientation. It is simply not enough for the partners and senior management of a firm to tell its employees that from now on they are going to behave and run the firm in a market-oriented manner. Simply producing a market orientation plan to be implemented by the employees of the firm is not sufficient to change organizational culture and in many cases can be counter-productive.

There is a management truism that holds that employees take notice of, and believe, what managers do rather than what they say. This is particularly apt in the case of creating a market-oriented culture in professional service firms. One particular firm that learned this lesson the hard and expensive way was an accountancy firm whose senior partner introduced a new client-centred service quality strategy into the firm. Having recognized the value of differentiating by service quality, and putting together a detailed quality programme, he held a series of meetings with all of the employees of the firm, from the receptionists and secretaries through to the partners, to unveil the new strategy complete with a client philosophy card for each person to carry with them at all times. While the firm was still 'buzzing' with the impact of the new strategy the senior partner was seen to violently disagree with a medium-sized client over some recent work undertaken, resulting in the partner telling the client to take his business elsewhere through the open door of his office as the client left. Needless to say the quality programme died on the spot as news of the incident spread throughout the firm and the time and expense involved in putting the strategy together were wasted. The firm believes what partners do, not what they say – the difference between lip-service and action is instantly recognizable to all employees.

Particular signs and signals will be discussed in more detail later in this chapter but amongst the most effective are recognition and reward systems and actions, marketing and communications training, market intelligence and marketing research, the status and role accorded to marketing, and measuring and using client quality evaluations. The signs and signals sent by senior managers and partners show the employees exactly what is felt to be important to those that own and manage the firm in the way they do their jobs and interact with clients. This is a far more powerful form of giving guidelines to staff about how to act and react than writing procedure manuals and sending memos.

Marketing skills

It has been argued here and elsewhere that all client contact and service provision staff are involved in the marketing of professional services.[6] This is particularly relevant in the context of achieving a market orientation. A market orientation exists primarily not in the minds of senior management and partners, nor in the written plans and strategies of the firm, but in the routine actions and behaviour of those who interact with, and provide service to, the clients of the professional service firm.

Once this basic truth about market orientation is realized then it becomes obvious that all client contact and service provision staff need to be furnished with 'marketing' skills which enable them to act and behave in a market-oriented manner. Skills that are likely to be particularly valuable include written and interpersonal communication skills, negotiating skills, marketing planning skills, presentation skills and even 'listening' skills.

Empowering client contact staff

If partners accept that two of the implicit components of a market orientation, and indeed marketing itself, in the professional service context, involve finding out precisely what a client needs and using the firm's resources and expertise to fulfil that client need, then it is impossible to ignore the critical role of client contact and service provision staff. Given the nature of the needs of most clients, it is likely that the precise nature of the professional service provided needs to be different for each client since the needs exhibited and problems faced by each client are unlikely to be exactly the same.

This has been recognized in the attempts of marketers to classify services in order to analyse how best to service market needs and plan marketing where professional services are generally regarded as requiring a very high degree of 'customization'.[7] The ability of client contact and service provision staff to customize the professional service offering is limited in many firms – particularly in medium and larger PSFs – by policy and procedure manuals and systems designed for management control purposes. While service marketers have proposed service standardization as one method of dealing with the characteristic heterogeneity of services as outlined in Chapter 1, this is an approach that can have the effect of limiting professionals' freedom to customize the firm's service offering and adapt it more specifically to the client's need in the professional service context.

It is important to realize that professional services do not only offer the opportunity to customize to a very high degree in theory, but that in reality clients also *expect* a very high degree of customization. In many cases it is very easy for clients to recognize a standardized approach to their problems and a standardized solution and this should not be underestimated as a source of client dissatisfaction and a predictor of clients losing confidence in the professional service provider.

Service provision and client contact staff are closer to the client, their problems and needs than anybody else in the firm. Partners and managers therefore need to remove the systems, procedures and 'norms' that form barriers to the complete customization of the service offering for each client. These barriers exist in even the most sophisticated professional service firm and can form severe and intractable obstacles to the achievement of a market orientation. While staff may be able to 'cheat the system' to a certain degree and on some occasions in order to deliver customized service to the client, they run the risk in many cases of being 'caught' and receiving negative 'brownie points' for acting in a market-oriented manner. This is clearly a situation where centralization and management controls actively militate against a market orientation.

The message here is simple, partners need to place trust in the client contact and service provision staff by removing the controls and systems that prevent them from acting in a market-oriented way.

Empower these people, cut them loose and the firm and its clients can benefit enormously.

Generating and sharing market intelligence

Of central importance in most modern definitions of market orientation is the requirement for the generation and dissemination of all kinds of information relating to the marketplace. The core of market intelligence is obviously information and research concerning current client needs but market intelligence also relates to information concerning future client needs, competitors and changes in the wider business environment – the type of information typically collected by environmental scanning systems allied with market research as described in Chapters 3 and 4. Market intelligence is not, however, necessarily a product of planned research and data collection and is certainly not the exclusive reserve of the marketing people. Market intelligence is likely to be acquired in various forms, informally as well as formally, by all of the staff of the firm, in all departments and across all functional areas. Thus conversations with clients of competitor firms at conferences, exchanges between students on training courses, even scouring the professional and trade press on a regular basis are as important as sources of market intelligence as formal market research.

However, simply collecting various types of information from diverse sources does not constitute market intelligence. In order to constitute market intelligence the information has to be analysed and interpreted and its implications for the firm, its clients and its competitors examined. Even this is not sufficient to achieve a market orientation in a professional service firm. It is not enough to use this information centrally – if a firm is to be responsive to market intelligence then it needs to share its market information with all of the firm's employees in order to keep staff aware of current marketplace needs and also to allow organization-wide interpretation of market information.

Professional service firms do not usually have advanced market intelligence systems and typically collect little market research and market information. In firms that do have formalized marketing information systems these are typically open only to people in senior management and marketing positions and not to 'front-line' employees. Many firms even go to the trouble of putting security codes into computer-based marketing information systems to restrict access. In firms without marketing information systems, the little market research undertaken and marketing information collected is typically restricted to the access of only a few senior professionals.

This situation directly contradicts the core of the market orientation construct. This is one problem area that professionals are typically reluctant to address primarily for budget reasons, a lack of confidence in providers of market research, and a fundamental distrust of the staff of the firms which they manage. The budget implications of market intelligence need not be as great as most professionals fear. As was discussed in Chapter 4, the problem within most professional service firms is not that they have too little market information but that they do not collate and use the market information that they have. Similarly, professionals need to be aware of the power of informal market intelligence dissemination through meetings, social interaction, etc. between the staff of the firm. This informal network system of intelligence collection and dissemination should be actively fostered and encouraged within professional service firms. Simple actions such as supporting regular social events, making meeting rooms, flip-charts, etc. available to staff at all times can produce the conditions that enable informal networking to flourish. This can also have an important impact upon inter-departmental relationships and information sharing which are important pre-conditions for the development of organization-wide responsiveness to market intelligence.

While attempting to reach the goals outlined above as a route to achieving a market orientation may seem a daunting prospect to many professional service firms, there are a set of skills, tools and resources which it is relatively easy to draw upon that can help firms to reach these goals.

Marketing training

Underlying the central idea of a market orientation is the notion that everybody in the firm needs to understand what marketing is and be committed to the idea of creating a responsive market-oriented firm. Unless this point is reached then the resistance to the changes implicit in creating a market-oriented firm will ensure that this goal is not achieved.

With this knowledge in mind, it is astounding that most marketers in professional service firms do very little (and in most cases no) marketing training amongst either partners or staff. In talking to many marketers about this particular problem it appears that most marketers within PSFs consider themselves unqualified and unsuited to 'teach' marketing and frequently abdicate responsibility to the training and development partner or function within the firm. Unfortunately, in most firms marketing training and education seems to fall between the marketing and training functions, with neither taking responsibility.

The obvious result of this is that the level of marketing training at all levels within professional service firms is almost negligible.

While many professionals would like simply to blame in-house marketers (where they exist) for abdicating responsibility for marketing training, we should remember that marketers are professionals just as accountants, lawyers, architects, engineers and doctors are professionals, and how many professionally qualified people are competent and confident enough to teach well? While there seems to be a problem with the source of marketing training there does not seem to be any problem at all with the demand side of the equation. I was recently asked to run a small marketing workshop in a very large city law firm to which the senior partner invited between twelve and fifteen partners. By the time I stood up to begin the workshop over ninety of the firm's staff had crowded into the room and all of them participated because they were interested, they felt it to be important and they had mostly heard about the event on the 'grapevine' – and had not been invited at all. Similarly, I recently gave a seminar in an accountancy firm at which I was to speak along with several other people from the firm itself. Having been scheduled to take the first 45 minutes of the seminar, the audience, and indeed the other speakers, did not let me sit down until nearly four hours later. The problem is not that professionals and staff are not interested in knowing more about marketing – the problem is that senior managers and professionals are not providing sources of training and education in marketing.

This is another opportunity for partners and senior managers to physically demonstrate to the whole of the firm that they believe that the development of a market orientation is important. Set time and budget aside for marketing training and education at all levels within the firm. This is particularly apt with partners and new recruits. Partners need to be able to fully understand marketing and market orientation if they are to demonstrate and communicate this to the rest of the firm. New recruits in terms of graduate trainees, etc. have yet to be exposed to the non-market-oriented firm and marketing training and education as a part of their induction courses and professional studies can help to ensure an incremental move towards a market-oriented firm.

One of the most formidable barriers to marketing training and education is the allocation of time – time that could be spent on fee-generating activities. Firms that I have worked with have demonstrated their commitment to achieving a market orientation by 'wasting' days and half-days on just such training and also running evening and weekend sessions. Budget need not be a huge obstacle to training since in-house seminars, workshops, etc. can be very cost-effective methods of marketing training and education.

Marketing planning

One of the most effective marketing training and development approaches that I have used with professional service firms is marketing planning exercises. This works particularly well in relatively marketing-unsophisticated firms. The idea is to use a workshop approach with a team of professionals to provide them with a basic framework and set of tools to put a strategic marketing plan together and take them through the planning process on a particular 'live' market that the firm is either currently serving or sees as a potential opportunity.

This approach has the advantage that it is very practical and 'hands-on' and it is explicitly concerned with marketing in the professional's own firm and usually produces some very tangible and useful output for the firm. Given a little more time this approach can also work effectively by taking a team of professionals through a 'dead' issue within the firm, e.g. a past new service introduction, a past new office opening, past marketing strategy, etc. as a first use of a rudimentary planning system before moving on to a 'live' project. The differences that emerge in the planning teams between how the dead project was handled, planned and executed at the time and the approaches that are suggested through the marketing planning process provide positive evidence for most professionals of the value of marketing planning – it has even led to the resurrection of dead projects with the new plan in some cases!

Any firm that does not engage in the rigorous and extensive training of all its staff in the philosophy, tools and techniques of marketing is missing an opportunity to demonstrate and communicate the importance of a market orientation. Even worse, it is leaving a substantial internal barrier to the achievement of an organization-wide responsiveness to market needs.

Internal marketing

Any marketer employed by any professional service firm who doesn't spend *at least* 50 per cent of their time, effort and budget on internal marketing, i.e. 'marketing' marketing and market orientation, to the partners, professionals and employees of the firm should be fired because they are not doing their job properly.

Marketers, whether they are full-blown marketing specialists or professionals with marketing responsibility, will typically need to spend many years after the introduction of marketing into a professional service firm getting all of the people within the organization to

194

accept and fulfil their role in the firm's marketing effort. This incremental culture change will *not* happen simply because the firm enjoys some external marketing success. Indeed, an isolated marketing function that is perceived as being successful without the fundamental involvement of partners and professional staff can actually be counterproductive since it allows the 'brass plaque' syndrome to receive support.

Marketers need to constantly create, find and exploit ways of increasing partnership and staff understanding of marketing, helping them to identify their individual and group marketing roles, giving them sufficient skills to fulfil these marketing roles, helping them find and interpret market information to which they can respond and, changing the outlook of professionals on the way the firm develops from a professional production orientation to a market responsiveness orientation. Any activity which is fundamentally aimed at creating one or more of these things *within* a firm may be labelled internal marketing. In many ways external marketing success cannot be long term until the above internal marketing targets have been achieved.

Most consultants and even some academics who have begun to talk about internal marketing are really only talking about internal communications. While internal marketing at the strategic level is certainly much more than this, there is a role for communications in the internal marketing mix. Indeed, almost anything that marketers can do to increase the information flows and two-way communications between individuals, departments, and up and down the organization's hierarchy is likely to improve its generation and dissemination of market intelligence and hence increase the likelihood of achieving a market orientation. However, merely concentrating upon the tactical communications element of the internal marketing mix ignores the potentially greater value of strategic internal marketing.[8]

At a strategic level we can view an internal marketing mix as applicable to all of the plans and strategies (including any plans or strategies to increase a market orientation) that are created, developed and written within the firm.[9] The strategic internal marketing approach forces firms to view their plans and strategies as 'products' that have to be marketed to an internal marketplace (the professionals and staff, even the partners within the firm) if they are to be successfully implemented. Thus we can view the internal marketing mix (Figure 11.1) as consisting of:

Product The strategy, plan or change we are trying to implement within the firm.
Price This consists of the physical cost of getting the plan implemented but is also the opportunity cost to the staff, i.e. what they

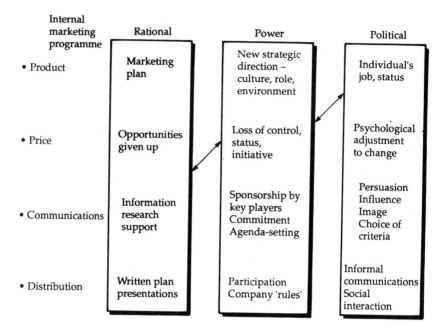

Figure 11.1 *Levels of internal marketing*

have to give up, put up with, etc. in order to implement this plan or strategy.

Communications   How we inform, change and communicate the plan (strategy) and change involved to the firm.

Distribution   Who we 'distribute' the plan/strategy/change to within the firm and through what 'channels', e.g. memos, written plans, presentations, partnership meetings, etc.

This conceptual model of strategic internal marketing has been developed further and has proven useful in dealing with implementation difficulties faced by planners in professional service firms, and indeed in many other types of commercial organization.[10] Simply applying marketing tools and techniques to the internal marketplace can be extremely productive. One of the great problems associated with introducing and implementing corporate or strategic marketing plans is that such plans and strategies are grounded in the analysis of external marketplaces that are both complex and rapidly changing. This means that the plans and strategies that we develop will usually call for some degree of internal change in order to react to, or anticipate, changes in the external marketplace.

196

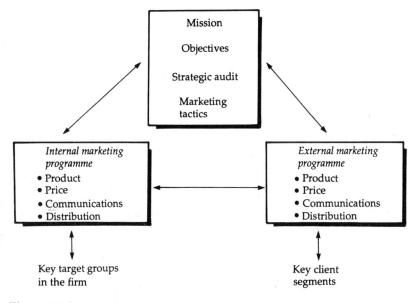

Figure 11.2

The reason that plans and strategies so often fail to be successfully implemented in professional service firms is not that they are necessarily 'bad' plans or strategies, but that their implementation calls for some degree of internal change and it is the *change* that is resisted by the professionals and employees – not the content of the plan or strategy itself. The strategic internal marketing framework can be useful in planning implementation strategies – as a part of the strategy formulation process, not as a 'bolt-on' at the end of it.

This framework can be particularly useful in anticipating implementation problems or barriers early on in the strategy formulation process when firms are planning market orientation strategies. Ideally, this framework should be 'institutionalized' in the formal planning system of the firm in the way outlined in Figure 11.2.

One of the most successful ways of reducing implementation problems is to make the people who will have to actually implement the plan, i.e. those whose behaviour, roles, jobs, etc. will have to change as a result of the plan or strategy developed, create and write the plan themselves. This can create the vital 'ownership' which is critical to making plans and strategies actually happen in organizations.

The internal marketing activities at both a tactical and strategic level can impact upon a professional service firm's ability to become market oriented and upon the successful implementation of plans and strategies that are designed to make a firm more market oriented. The strategic internal marketing framework is particularly useful in terms of strategic marketing and corporate planning in the case of a firm that wishes to become market oriented. Actually achieving a market orientation means that a firm is committed to being responsive throughout its organization to changes in the marketplace and business environment. Since the evidence is that the marketplaces and business environment for professional service firms are becoming ever more complex and changing with increasing rapidity, then a commitment to a market orientation is a commitment to regular internal change within the firm. Market orientation in these terms is a form of continuous change and innovative behaviour within professional service firms. Thus strategic internal marketing as a framework for managing internal change is vital in both achieving and implementing a market orientation.

Market intelligence systems

There are a whole host of relatively simple tools and techniques in the areas of marketing research, environmental scanning and marketing information systems that we can use to create market intelligence systems. While firms should do everything possible to encourage and increase internal networking and the sharing of market intelligence, a simple formalized market intelligence system should not necessarily interface with or decrease informal activities.

A simple formalized intelligence system could include: departmental environmental scanning exercises on a regular basis in departmental teams with the output shared both within and between departments; regular sharing and widespread dissemination of any marketing research undertaken by the firm amongst all departments and staff with follow-up meetings at all levels to discuss the implications of the research and possible organization-wide responses to it; much more widespread use and updating of client files capturing more related information about the client than simply the work done and the fees charged; and the simplification of computer-based marketing information systems and databases with sharing encouraged on an organization-wide basis and easy access (particularly in terms of passwords and entry codes, etc.).

While these resources involve considerable time and effort on the part of many within the firm they are not necessarily expensive in terms of budget and the skills, tools and techniques can be quickly learned and, more importantly, demonstrated via a routinization of the system.

Strategies for achieving a market orientation

We simply do not have the longitudinal studies to enable a prescriptive generic strategy for achieving a market orientation in a professional service firm (or indeed any other form of commercial organization) to be constructed. What we do know, however, is that strategies and plans created, developed and written by the senior management of a firm are more likely to run into implementation failures and difficulties, than those created by the people who will actually have to implement the plan or strategy.

We also know that for the vast majority of professional service firms the achievement of a market orientation is likely to involve structural, process, cultural and systems change within the firm – all of which are likely to be resisted to a greater or lesser degree by the partners, professionals and staff of the firm. Each of the changes implicit in a market orientation are likely to challenge the 'status quo' and thus the power positions of individuals, departments and functions within the firm, and will thus be resisted by anyone who feels they will 'lose out' as a result of the changes.

The role of the top management of the firm in actively creating a market orientation within the firm may therefore be much more limited than they would like or expect. Narver and Slater contrasted the two basic approaches to strategies for achieving a market orientation as top-down and bottom-up strategies (Figure 11.3) and concluded that their effectiveness over a short period of time was likely to be inversely related.

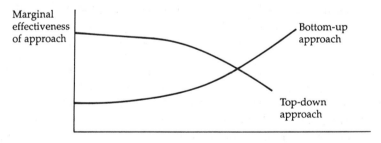

Figure 11.3 *Market orientation strategy approach*

It would seem that the best approach to achieving a market orientation in a professional service firm is likely to be a combination top-down/bottom-up approach.

There are two major roles for the top management in this approach to developing a market orientation. First, they have to educate the partners, professionals and staff of the firm in terms of basic comprehension of a market orientation and what it involves, and convince them that the firm does have an existing or potential problem to which a market orientation may provide some answers. Thus the entire firm has to be made to understand market orientation and to recognize what potentially it can achieve for the firm and everybody working within it.

Second, top management have to remove the barriers to achieving a market orientation that their present organization, management systems, roles and procedures create. This can be viewed as a combination of concrete actions that both send demonstrable cultural signals about the importance of a market orientation and the commitment to it at a senior level, and a movement to empower the service provision and client contact front-line staff to use their client knowledge, and the opportunity of regular interaction with the client to customize the service offering and delivery, to ensure the maximum satisfaction of client needs.

Once these two roles of top management have been achieved then partners, professionals and staff should be actively encouraged to formulate their own plans and strategies for developing a market orientation within their own sections, functions, departments, markets, etc. This will involve giving everybody some rudimentary planning skills, time and budget for planning teams and time, effort and ultimately budget to review and implement the resulting plans. Having been given guidelines in terms of time-frame, budget and general direction from top management, the chosen organizational units should be allowed to produce and implement their own strategies for developing, achieving and increasing their market orientation.

This mix of top-down/bottom-up in approaching strategies for achieving a market orientation is more costly in terms of time and effort spent in planning and developing the market orientation strategy but is far more effective in avoiding implementation failures and difficulties and actually achieving a market orientation to a greater degree and in a shorter space of time.

I always hesitate to give advice along the lines of 'the best strategy for achieving this is . . .'. One of the conclusions that my co-researcher Nigel Piercy and I have been increasingly driven towards in our work over the past three or four years is that the bulk of strategic management literature and the activities of strategy consultants is largely built upon the notion of finding an 'optimum' strategy through the use of ever more complex models, tools and techniques. We have come to the conclusion that there is no such thing as an optimum

Figure 11.4

strategy in any given environment or organization, there is only the strategy that your organization, with its current capabilities and constraints, with its existing structures, systems, processes and people, is best capable of actively implementing and delivering into the marketplace (see Figure 11.4).

In terms of strategy formulation we are therefore far better off creating simple plans that match up with all the capabilities and constraints of our firm, and taking into account the 'needs' of the internal 'marketplace', that we can actually implement and deliver into the marketplace, than creating 'optimum' computer modelled, laser printed, colour co-ordinated, leather bound plans which are perfect in terms of strategy formulation *vis-à-vis* a particular market but are never likely to get implemented. This is particularly true in terms of strategies for creating a market orientation within a professional service firm – it is more effective to allow your staff to create 'mediocre' plans for market orientation which they go out and implement, than for top management to create 'perfect' plans for achieving a market orientation which never get implemented.

In situations in which the top management of a firm either faces so much potential resistance to achieving a market orientation that little is likely to happen, or conversely in situations in which a few individuals only are committed to 'making marketing happen' then a 'chunking' approach may be necessary.

This simply entails taking a small and discrete unit of the firm's business, such as one client service group or one department, and introducing and implementing a market orientation within this one unit. I have used this approach in several firms and the power of demonstration and the interest, excitement and enthusiasm that it can cause amongst the rest of the firm are often powerful enough to drive a bottom-up movement towards a market orientation within the whole of the firm.

Developing a market orientation is certainly not a panacea. However, it is increasingly becoming a competitive imperative. A market orientation cannot be achieved in a professional service firm quickly, easily or without considerable internal change and thus internal pain. The consequences of a market orientation and the realities of the new competition in professional services marketplaces do, however, mean that all PSFs will have to address this issue if they wish to survive in the long term, and perform even adequately in the medium term.

References

1 Carson, D. (1968), 'Marketing organisation in British manufacturing firms', *Journal of Marketing*, vol. 32, pp. 35–39.

2 Ames, C. B. (1970), 'Trappings vs. substance in industrial marketing', *Harvard Business Review*, July/August, pp. 93–102.

3 Kohli, A. K. and Jaworski, B. J. (1990), 'Market orientation: the construct, research propositions and managerial implications', *Journal of Marketing*, vol. 54, no. 2, pp. 1–19.

4 Jaworski, B. J. and Kohli, A. K. (1990), 'Market orientation: understanding the antecedents and consequences', paper presented at Marketing Science Institute conference, *Organizing to Become Market-Driven*, Boston, Mass, Sept; Narver, J. and Slater, S. (1990), 'Strategies for increasing a market orientation', paper presented at Marketing Science Institute conference, *Organizing to Become Market-Driven*, Boston, Mass, Sept 1990

5 Kohli, A. K. and Jaworski, B. J. (1990), op. cit.

6 Morgan, N. A. (1990), 'Barriers to implementing marketing in professional service firms', *Marketing Education Group Conference*, Oxford.

7 Lovelock, C. H. (1983), 'Classifying services to gain strategic marketing insights', *Journal of Marketing*, vol. 47, Summer, pp. 9–20.

8 Piercy, N. F. and Morgan, N. A. (1989), 'Good plans need internal marketing', *Sunday Times*, 10 September.

9 Morgan, N. A. (1900), 'Implementing marketing: Key issues for professional service firms', *Journal of Professional Services Marketing*, vol. 6, no. 1 Fall.

10 Piercy, N. F. and Morgan. N. A. (1990), 'Internal marketing as leverage for market-led strategic change', *Irish Marketing Review*, vol. 4, no. 3, pp. 11–29.

11 Narver, J. C. and Slater, S. F. (1990), op. cit.

12 Marketing and quality

At first glance many readers may wonder why this book includes a chapter on marketing and quality, in such an important position. There is an uncomplicated reason for its inclusion – quality is potentially the greatest lever that exists for marketers and marketing, both within a professional services firm and in the competitive marketplace for professional services. The reasons for this, if not immediately obvious, will become clear in this chapter. The actual nature of the relationship between marketing and quality is as yet a relatively underdeveloped topic. However, even a rudimentary analysis can uncover for the professional service marketer a wealth of opportunities.

The issue of quality in its various guises moved to the top of the management agenda in all kinds of commercial organizations in the Western World throughout the 1980s. The quality 'movement' began as a response to Japanese competition amongst US manufacturing organizations and was subsequently imported into UK manufacturing industry. In the service sector the USA has again played the lead role in the development and application of quality programmes. The service sector in the UK is only really just beginning to think about the quality issue and the role that it might play in service businesses. The professional service sector has not been in the forefront of this movement in the UK although some firms are beginning to at least raise the quality issue internally.

In considering the quality issue in the professional service context one of the responses that is initially exhibited is – well we offer a very high quality service anyway, so why should we waste time, money, effort, etc. on quality programmes. Answering the question 'why is quality important in the professional service sector?' is difficult to do given the lack of empirical work in this particular area. However, work from other sectors and my own observations and research can give some insight.

Perhaps the most immediate and obvious argument for taking a serious look at the quality issue in professional service firms, irrespective of whether or not you believe your firm has a quality problem, is the costs of ignoring it. Some estimates from quality experts in the UK indicate that there is a physical cost associated with producing a service that is perceived by clients as being 'on a par with competitors' of as much as 30–40 per cent[1] of total fee income! Even in small professional service firms over one-third of potential fee income is not achieved due to 'average' service quality. These are estimates of the extra potential fee income that may be available to service businesses providing a service that is perceived by clients to be of a higher quality than competing firms can achieve. Such potentially large implications upon fee income, and in turn partnership funds, makes service quality an expensive issue to ignore and one that has potentially an enormous impact not only upon the growth and profitability of the firm but also, at the end of the day, the wealth of individual partners – a matter close to the heart of most professionals!

Further evidence of a relationship between quality, return on investment and market share has been provided by the respected PIMS database in the USA. Many professionals will have received through the management literature the message from the PIMS work that market share is related to profitability. Few professionals have gone further than this basic message, for much of the PIMS work has centred upon quality. The findings on quality are startling.[2] The first finding is that, while market share is related to profit, sustainable market share itself comes from 'relative perceived product or service quality'. Further, the PIMS researchers found that in their database of 4000 US business units, relative quality i.e. quality relative to that of competitors, is the single most important factor in the long-term performance of a business unit.

PIMS researchers also looked at the question of value. This is particularly apposite in the professional service context where 'adding value' for clients seems to have become the objective of most professional service firm growth strategies. Value is not a difficult concept to consider – it is essentially the trade-off between price and quality. There are therefore two basic ways in which PSFs can add value for clients (i) lower fee levels and thus client costs (ii) raise service quality so that the client perceives more service for the same fees. In terms of value, the PIMS research indicates that client perceptions of value are more effectively changed by raising service quality than by lowering fee levels and service costs.

Given the potential implications of quality in professional services in terms of client value, fee income and ultimately partnership profitability, the management of client quality perceptions may be viewed as the most important task facing professional service firms in the 1990s.

Quality is regarded as a fundamental, but largely implicit, issue in most professions. This is reflected in the very nature of the professional bodies which are largely concerned with the quality control of their membership by education and examination prior to qualification, and continuing education, codes of conduct and directives, and the ultimate power of veto on an individual professional's membership of the professional body. It is also considered a largely implicit issue within professional service firms themselves. One of the commonest questions that I pose to PSFs is 'In what way does your firm differentiate itself from its major competitors?' In the large majority of cases – after an initial stunned silence, indicating that this is not a question that has ever been explicitly asked within the firm before – the reply usually runs along the lines of 'we offer a high quality service.' As was discussed in Chapter 8, differentiating on the basis of quality is certainly a credible option to be considered in most professional service marketplaces. There are, however, two problems with differentiating upon quality in this context. First, the underlying rationale for differentiation is to achieve competitive advantage through making a PSF different from its generic competitors. If most PSFs are attempting to differentiate themselves upon the same basis, i.e. quality, then it makes it very difficult for individual PSFs to obtain a client perception that they are different from their competitors. The second problem is, if anything, even more fundamental. When professionals talk about quality of professional services they are almost always talking about technical issues. To most professionals quality means having the best technical and professional service offering – the best litigators, engineers, auditors, consultants. This is, however, only one part, and probably the *least* important aspect of professional service quality.

What is quality?

As with most such questions about important issues there is no clearly defined and widely accepted definition of what quality actually is. In essence the concept of quality has been viewed, at least in the academic world, as the difference between expectations and the perception of outcomes.[3] In the professional service context this can be modelled in a very simple way,[4] as shown in Figure 12.1.

Thus in the simplest terms perceived quality is the difference

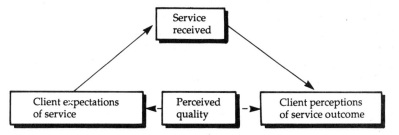

Figure 12.1 *Model of professional service quality*

between what a client expects of, and from, a professional service and how the client perceives that the received professional service lived up to those expectations. If perceptions of outcome match initial client expectations exactly then the client will be satisfied. If perceptions of outcome are greater than prior expectation then the client will perceive a higher quality service, while if perceptions of outcome are lower than expectations then the client will have a low quality perception and is likely to be unsatisfied.

In terms of what quality actually means in the 'real' as opposed to the 'academic' world there are no shortage of quality definitions. Figure 12.2 contains the definitions of quality used by the 'gurus' of the worldwide quality movement.

'Conformance to requirements'
Philip Crosby

'Predictable degree of uniformity and dependability at low cost and suited to the market'
Dr E. Deming

'Fitness for purpose'
Joe Juan

'Meeting the customer requirements'
John Oakland

Figure 12.2 *Quality definitions*

The views of the 'gurus' and consultants are therefore surprisingly close to those of academics. The views largely converge upon the central overriding notion that quality is not an absolute concept and that its importance comes only in terms of client perceptions – therefore it is the client's perception of the quality of the outcome of, and from, a service that is important. The reality of the outcome of the service as far as the professional service provider is concerned is unimportant. The focus for all discussion and action upon quality and professional services has to be upon client perceptions.

This central notion in the quality issue forms the first of the stumbling blocks for marketing and marketers in the professional service context. To partners and professionals in PSFs service quality is essentially a product of technical expertise and professional guidelines. Thus the focus in professionals own understanding of quality is internal and related to technical and professional issues and not external and focused upon client expectations and managing perceptions of outcome. This gap between what professionals believe that clients evaluate in developing their quality perception and the criteria that clients *actually* use in evaluating service quality is in most cases vast. Thus even firms that have installed quality assurance systems or total quality management programmes may be largely wasting time and effort unless the thrust of their actions is based upon the real criteria that are used by clients to evaluate service quality.

The problem that faces even those PSFs that recognize this is that we actually know very little about how clients arrive at a perception of quality. Some academics have suggested that clients, in reaching a quality evaluation of a professional service, do not only evaluate the outcome of the service performed but also evaluate the process, i.e. the service delivery and interaction with service provision staff.[5] Research has been undertaken in the USA that has produced a new and widely accepted set of criteria used by consumers of a number of services outside the professional service sector.[6] This research proposes that consumers of services evaluate the quality of the service they receive and its outcome on ten quality dimensions:

1 *Reliability* revolving around consistency and dependability, particularly in terms of delivering on promises.
2 *Responsiveness* involving the willingness, readiness and time-liness of service provision.
3 *Competence* referring to the skills and ability of the service provision and contact staff.
4 *Access* this criteria involves not only ease of contact but general approachability.
5 *Courtesy* involves consideration, politeness and even friendli-ness of staff.
6 *Communication* this criteria involves communication both ways, communicating clearly and regularly with clients and also listen-ing to clients.
7 *Credibility* this involves honesty, trustworthiness, believability and reputation.
8 *Security* this primarily means freedom from doubt, risk or even danger.
9 *Knowing/understanding the customer* the level of effort made to fully understand the client's need and the customizing of service on the basis of this knowledge.
10 *Tangibles* these are tangible elements such as physical facilities and equipment and personal appearance of service provision and client contact staff.

While these determinants of quality perceptions are from research in non-professional service businesses they do begin to provide a framework that can be used internally to focus professionals' minds upon potential client quality evaluation criteria, and even as a basic measurement tool for building a professional services quality determination model. The first point that has to be forcefully made to any firm in considering quality is that any effective approach to managing client quality perceptions has to operate upon issues which are *actually* important to clients and the criteria that clients *do* use to evaluate quality, rather than upon issues which professionals *think* are important to clients and the criteria that *partners* use to evaluate quality.

There have been some initial efforts to relate the notion of service quality in the professionals service context in terms of uncovering criteria used by clients in evaluating service quality and their relative importance. In the USA one academic study by Jackson, Brown and Keith in 1984 produced the results shown in Table 12.1.

Table 12.1 *Importance of various factors in evaluating a law firm*

Factors	Mean*
Results of firm's work	1.11
Counsel and advice	1.17
Expertise in specific area	1.25
Personal interest in client's legal matters	1.28
Quality of written product	1.34
Keeping client informed of firm's progress	1.44
Verbal skills	1.48
Fast turnaround on work	1.52
Personal interest taken in client's business	1.72
Access to top people in the firm	1.79
The firm's reputation in the community	1.80
Ability to work with a specific lawyer	1.89
Representation of similar clients	2.62
Low cost	2.72
Size of firm	2.86
Location of firm's offices	2.96
Political connections	3.20

*Means for response 1 = very important
                       5 = very unimportant
Source: Jackson, D. W., Brown, S. W. and Keith, J. E. 'Business executive evaluations of various aspects of outside legal services', in Block, T., Upah, G. and Zeithaml, V., *Services Marketing in a Changing Environment*, Chicago: AMA.

This work demonstrates the use of both outcome and process criteria in the quality evaluation process of organizational clients as well as consumer clients.

My own exploratory research in this area has also concentrated upon organizational clients of law firms. A survey of 168 corporate clients yielded the results shown in Table 12.2 in terms of evaluation of various aspects of client service – with the measures themselves being constructed from existing academic literature and adapted to the professional service context.

Table 12.2 *Evaluation of client service levels*

Factor	Mean*
Partners provide individual attention	1.40
Firm takes prompt action when problems arise	1.52
Perform services dependably and accurately	1.53
Respond rapidly to our enquiries	1.60
All staff improve confidence	1.73
Obviously rate client service highly	1.75
Work to our deadlines rather than their own	1.78
Have staff who communicate well	1.81
Charge reasonable fees	2.10
Keep us informed of progress without us having to ask	2.12
Anticipate our legal services needs	2.67
Ask us how they can serve us better	3.12

*Means for responses when 1 = True, 5 = False

Table 12.3 *Dimensions of client service quality*

1	Problem solving creativity	looking beyond the obvious and not being bound by accepted professional and technical approaches
2	Initiative	includes anticipating problems and opportunities and not just reacting
3	Efficiency	keeping client costs down through effective work planning and control
4	Fast response	responding to enquiries, questions, problems as quickly as possible
5	Timeliness	starting and finishing service work to agreed deadlines
6	Open-mindedness	professionals not being 'blinkered' by their technical approach
7	Sound judgement	clients want business advice not just accounting advice
8	Functional expertise	need to bring together all the functional skills necessary from whatever sources to work on a client project
9	Industry expertise	clients expect professionals to be thoroughly familiar with their industry and recent changes in it
10	Managerial effectiveness	maintaining a focus upon the use of both the firm's and the client's resources
11	Orderly work approach	clients expect salient issues to be identified early and do not want last minute surprises before deadlines
12	Commitment	clients evaluate the calibre of the accountant and the individual attention given
13	Long-range focus	clients prefer long-term relationships rather than 'projects' or 'jobs'
14	Qualitative approach	accountants should not be seen as simple number crunchers
15	Continuity	clients do not like firms who constantly change the staff that work with them – they will evaluate staff continuity as part of ongoing relationship
16	Personality	clients will also evaluate the friendliness, understanding and co-operation of the service provider

Source: *Marketing News*, 28 May 1990.

Further work has recently been undertaken in the USA by Deloitte & Touche[7] based upon interviews with over 500 corporate clients of accountancy firms. This research into criteria which clients actually used in evaluating service quality generated sixteen dimensions of client service quality. These are listed in Table 12.3 in order of priority.

Most readers will by now have begun to grasp something of the essential nature of the relationship between quality management and marketing. There is potentially such an important overlap between quality and marketing that it is worth explaining this relationship further.

One of the most important features of this relationship is the process by which clients arrive at a quality evaluation of a professional service. This process may be modelled as shown at Figure 12.3.

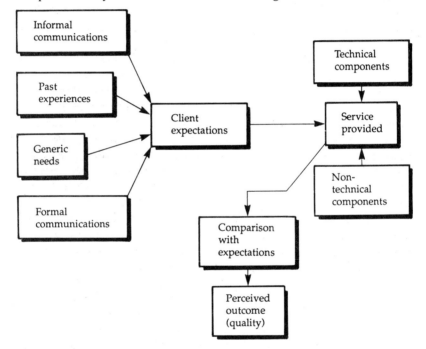

Figure 12.3 *The quality evaluation process*

This model of the quality evaluation process illustrates the potentially enormous role that marketing can play in managing quality perceptions. On the expectations side of the quality equation the marketing function can actively participate in the quality evaluation process in a number of important ways.

Marketing research tools and techniques can and should be used to uncover both generic needs and past experiences as components, and overall client expectations as a composite of both technical and process client expectations. Marketing communications programmes can be designed to actively manage these components that feed into client expectations – formal communications such as promotional literature and advertisements that give clients some idea of reasonable expectations, and informal communications strategies based around word-of-mouth, referral sources and public relations. In terms of the actual service provided, marketing obviously has a role to play in the service development process providing not only generic needs information around which the technical aspects of the service offering can be formulated but also the other, and perhaps more important, aspects of expectations that are non-technical such as client/professional communications, timing and delivery of service, appropriate fee schedules, etc.

Marketing may also have a role to play in the post service-delivery phase of the client quality-evaluation process by working to manipulate client perceptions of the outcome and the process of the professional service. This may be achieved primarily through both one and two-way communications – one-way communication aimed at reassuring the client that the technical service outcome has fulfilled their needs, i.e. communications that tell clients that they chose the 'right' professional service supplier, and also two-way communications in terms of the face-to-face opportunity provided by the signing-off of a project or phase of work, and in more forward thinking firms by a formal client satisfaction system, in which clients are asked 'Just how well did we do?' and 'Is there any way that we can improve the way we serve clients?' Simply giving clients an opportunity to moan, complain, whinge and gripe about our service provision can, in itself, improve client perceptions of oucomes and allow clients to 'let off steam' long before any dissatisfaction leads to them changing firms.

The marketing function may therefore be seen not only to have a vital role to play in any professional service quality programme but also to have the necessary tools and techniques to fulfil this role. In the manufacturing sector the total quality management movement has failed to achieve its potential in the large majority of organizations. One of the reasons for this relative failure is that a narrow view of what quality is has been adopted, and the whole quality management process has become driven either by specialist quality staff functions with directors of quality, quality managers, etc., or by the engineering and production functions. This form of quality management is driven by statistical process control of production. In terms of the concept of quality, this approach can only impact upon the outcome side of the quality equation – and only upon the reality of the outcome, not the customer perception of that reality. It ignores the expectations side of the quality equation almost completely.

While the quality management concept is still relatively new ground in the professional services context it is important that it is not approached in the same way as it has been by both manufacturing organizations and also by the professional bodies. The main professional bodies in the UK seem concerned with quality only in the technical outcomes sense of the term – and it is therefore driven by standards committees, etc. Those professional bodies that have thought about quality even more explicitly by producing quality guidelines for individuals and member firms, such as the RICS guidelines on quality assurance, take the same approach and singularly avoid any notion that quality has the remotest relationship with client expectations. The RICS guidelines concentrate upon minimizing physical risk from surveying services.[8]

For quality to be successful in achieving its potential in the professional service context it needs to be viewed in its widest sense, encompassing both sides of the quality equation, and it needs to be driven by those with marketing skills rather than professionals with technical skills. Professional technical quality does have a role to play in service quality programmes but it is a minor role and does not necessitate quality becoming an issue for technical specialists. A quality committee consisting of technical and ethical specialists is not a quality committee at all, it is a technical committee. While quality is still a new issue in the professional service context, and is still seen as an issue that is difficult for professional service firms to deal with, the opportunity exists for marketers and marketing-oriented professionals to take the lead. If your firm has yet to fully grasp the quality nettle make sure that the marketing function is seen to take the lead in working parties, pilot programmes, workshops, etc.

What is required in PSFs, and is currently absent in most firms, is a coherent quality strategy. A professional service quality strategy is likely to involve:

1 Marketing research through interviews, focus groups, etc. in order to define the criteria used by clients to evaluate the quality of a professional service offering. This information should be examined for differences across existing segments of the client base, and the possibility of using this information as the basis of a benefit segmentation analysis should be closely examined. This will allow the firm to define, in client terms, service quality for each of its market segments.

2 Critical to the successful planning and implementation of a professional service quality strategy is the commitment of the senior partners and management of the firm[9] – both as a resource base and as providers of signals to professional and client contact

staff of key values within the firm. Commitment of senior people has to be achieved for the long term. Quality strategies are not, and cannot be, 'one off' programmes for improving service quality. The whole quality process, by its nature, is an ongoing process and is often pictured as a wheel of quality which needs to be continuously turned.[10] A PSF needs a commitment to quality in the long run, because that is the way quality works. Anything less is lip-service. One useful mechanism for gaining senior management commitment to a quality strategy is gap analysis.

Gap analysis in this context refers to the gaps that exist between the criteria used to evaluate PSFs internally by professionals and managers, and externally by clients.[11] Tacking on some 'internal research', stage 1 of the quality strategy above can give a powerful weapon to be used by those championing the quality issue to move senior management to the 'problem recognition' stage. An implicit and explicit recognition of the importance of quality, not in the abstract, but in the context of their own firm and clients, is an essential pre-condition to the implementation of any serious quality strategy.

3 As with most successful planning activities, the planning of the firm's quality strategy needs a bottom-up, team-based approach. With the information from the research telling us the criteria upon which clients evaluate quality we will need to re-examine the design of our professional service offering and the way in which it is delivered. Marketing research can again be useful at this stage. Having uncovered the criteria used in client quality evaluations, further research can be useful in terms of highlighting the areas in which the firm is failing to meet client expectations. This can provide priority objectives for our quality planning teams in their approach to redesigning service content and delivery based upon client quality evaluation criteria and client perceived quality problems with our service. In cases where PSFs encounter particular problems with a service offering it may be worthwhile considering the systems-based 'blueprinting' approach advocated by G. Lynn Shostack which can be useful and provide insights into the radical redesign of service with the emphasis upon how the service is physically produced and delivered to the client.[12]

The bottom-up, participative planning approach is also of particular use in this context since it forces professionals, service providers and client contact staff, i.e. everybody, to face the fact that a commitment to quality necessitates the active involvement of every single employee of the firm. It is difficult to abdicate responsibility for quality to 'The Quality Committee', or 'Management Committee' when you are actively involved in planning the quality programme actions and activities for your department, section, clients or whatever. It is also an effective mechanism for gaining the ownership of quality problems and commitment to quality solutions that are vital for the implementation of a quality strategy.

4 The problem with bottom-up planning is that it can become difficult to manage. After one very successful bottom-up based planning assignment the firm's senior partner commented 'This is like riding on the back of tiger!' Once you have a departmental team or whatever unit energized and enthusiastic about their plans you have to give them the support and resource they need to implement them. If this necessitates taking twenty clients to lunch to test out some new ideas, a full-blown communications skills training course for every member of the department, three new phone lines and a new secretary in a department or whatever, the management of the firm have to sensibly resource quality plans. Philip Crosby's *Quality is Free* is a good book for manufacturers but its title is misleading. Quality is not free and managing client quality perceptions can be expensive in the short term. The rewards in terms of client loyalty, enhanced reputation, additional cross-selling and ultimately new clients, will not appear until the medium-long term. Quality is *not* free. Quality *is* an investment.

As with marketing planning teams, if we are to avoid quality planning teams asking for unrealistically high investment in their plans we need to ensure a constant iteration between the team and the management and to be very specific in terms of the brief we give the team.

5 If the firm is serious about a commitment to quality it will systematically measure quality perceptions. Measuring client quality perceptions is never going to be an exact science but it doesn't have to be. In most PSFs, quality programmes will be aiming for improvements upon base scores in terms of orders of magnitudes not in terms of a second decimal point. However you decide to measure quality perceptions the measures have to continue to be based upon client quality evaluation criteria and therefore may be different across different segments of the firm's client base. Whatever measurement device is utilized, i.e. survey, telephone interview, focus group, etc., the results need to be shared with everyone in the firm. Some partners may object to this on the basis of internal competition being unproductive. The thought of having the problem of managing departments or even individual partners and professionals competing upon who can best serve the client's needs is one that most senior partners can learn to live with, and most marketing partners would give their right arm for!

If everyone in the firm is to take the quality strategy seriously then quality perception measures and results should feed not only into the quality programme but into the evaluation and reward system for the employees and members of the firm. Staff compensation, evaluating for promotion and assessing staff personal training and development needs based upon client quality perceptions is enough to convince even the most die-hard cynic that the firm is serious in its commitment to quality. It is this cultural signal that will provide the impetus to not only put together a quality programme to begin with, but ensure that the 'wheel of quality' is turned not once, but continuously.

Most readers will by now have grasped the importance of quality in the marketing of professional services. It provides an important weapon in the development of a market orientation within firms; a particularly vital weapon in firms that have 'anti-marketing' values and professional cultures. In many cases it may prove easier to convince partners of the true meaning and role of quality than of marketing. If this is the case in your firm then marketers and professionals should be unafraid of becoming quality managers, quality directors or quality partners. You will still be performing the role which marketing can perform – in essence it is simply a case of changing the label to suit the culture.

In most firms, however, quality need not become an 'alternative' to marketing but an addition to marketing. Marketers within PSFs need to grasp the opportunity afforded to them by the emergence of the quality issue, to take the lead in introducing and running quality programmes. This can lead to an increase in the internal 'clout' of marketing with the professionals in the firm and can also effectively reduce many of the barriers to making marketing 'happen' described in Chapter 11.

References

1 Oakland, J. (1989), *Total Quality Management*, Oxford: Butterworth-Heinemann.
2 Buzzell, R. D. and Gale, R. T. (1987), *The PIMS Principles – Linking Strategy to Performance*, New York: Free Press.
3 Parasuraman, A., Zeithaml, V. A. and Berry, L. L. (1988), 'SERQUAL: a multiple item scale for measuring consumer perceptions of service quality', *Journal of Retailing*, vol. 64, no. 1, Spring.
4 Morgan, N. A. (1990), 'Quality and marketing in professional service firms', *Professional Practice Development*, vol. 2, no. 1, March.
5 Lehtinen, U. and Lehtinen, J. R. (1982), 'Service quality: a study of

quality dimensions', unpublished working paper, Helsinki: Service Management Institute, Finland, OY; Gronroos, C. (1984), 'A service quality model and its marketing implications', *European Journal of Marketing*, vol. 18, no. 4, pp. 36–44.

6 Parasuraman, A., Zeithaml, V. A. and Berry, L. L. (1985), 'A conceptual model of service quality and its implications for future research', *Journal of Marketing*, vol. 49, Fall, pp. 41–50.

7 Lynch, B. K. (1990), 'Creative problem solving heads list of service priorities', *Marketing News*, 28 May, p. 24.

8 Royal Institute for Chartered Surveyors (1989), *Quallity Assurance*, London: RICS, January.

9 Haywood-Farmer, J. (1986), 'Controlling service quality', *Business Quarterly*, vol. 50, no. 4, pp. 62–67; Alberecht, K. and Zemke, R. (1985), 'Instilling a service mentality: like teaching an elephant to dance', *International Management*, November, pp. 61–67.

10 Heskett, J. L. (1987), 'Lessons in the service sector', *Harvard Business Review*, vol. 65, March–April, pp. 118–126.

11 Brown, S. W. and Swartz, T. A. (1989), 'A gap analysis of professional service quality', *Journal of Marketing*, vol. 53, no. 2, April, pp. 92–99.

12 Shostack, L. G. (1987), 'Service positioning through structural change', *Journal of Marketing*, vol. 51, January, pp. 34–43.

should not be underestimated. Alongside the size and significance of the changes necessary to develop a market orientation is the truly astounding ability of most partners and professionals, in most professional service firms, to resist change. It is even possible to view partners and professionals as substantially better at not doing things they *don't* want to than at doing the things that they *do*.

This internal resistance to change is the biggest single obstacle that marketers in professional service firms face. Even more difficult is the fact that while internal marketing is primarily aimed at 'marketing' marketing to partners, key decision makers, professionals and staff, the goal of achieving a market orientation is not a static one. If creating a market-oriented PSF is essentially about getting the entire firm to respond to existing and anticipated client needs, then an additional problem is that increasingly client needs are changing, not over periods measured in decades or years, but in terms of months, weeks and even days. Thus a market orientation means constantly changing what a professional service firm does, and the way that it does it, in response to client needs.

The task of marketing development may therefore be even more difficult and complex than it appears on the surface. What marketers are actually trying to get senior partners and managers initially, and all the firm's staff eventually, to 'buy' is a series of radical changes in their working lives which will be continuous, if irregular, as a response to changing market needs.

Thus the goal may be seen to be creating a recognition of the need for change within professional service firms and getting whole firms to embrace and even enjoy constant change in what they do and the way that they do it. Unsurprisingly, perhaps, given the magnitude of this goal, there are no quick-fix, off-the-shelf, answers. Even gaining a recognition of this goal is difficult enough in most professional service firms.

There are a number of specific obstacles and problems that are apparent in attempting to achieve the overall goal. It is these problems that make marketing in the professional service context different from marketing in other commercial sectors. Professional services marketing is certainly different from marketing Mars bars or soap powder. Many marketers who have attempted to use and translate their marketing skills and experience from product marketing, and even services marketing in other sectors, have found the difficulties and peculiarities of the professional service context to be unique. Amongst these, particular differences relate to:

13 Conclusions

All of the research work in the area of professional services marketing, along with the experiences of consultants, marketers and professionals highlights that there remains a substantial gap between what marketing can potentially achieve in the professions, and the reality of what marketing is actually achieving in the management and development of professional service firms. Professional service firms still see marketing as a 'distress purchase' in the face of an increasingly competitive business environment rather than an opportunity to change the way they service market needs and achieve long-term competitive advantage. This gap is perhaps most starkly seen in the responsibilities accorded in-house marketers and the stubborn resistance of the vast majority of professionals to recognize and accept their own roles in the firm's marketing efforts.

The harsh reality which has to be faced by all those involved in professional services marketing is that this gap is unlikely to be closed until senior partners, management committees and all those responsible for actually managing professional service firms are committed to developing market-oriented firms. To date, professionals with such responsibility have largely paid lip-service to the goal of market orientation within their firms.

Lip-service is not only a problem for those managing PSFs, it is also a problem for the rest of the firm. Even if it remains unrecognizable to senior partners and managers, lip-service is easily recognized by the professionals and staff within professional service firms. Sending memos, giving seminars, developing plans and appointing in-house marketers is still viewed as an abdication of responsibility and a substitute for positive action by professionals and staff.

Senior management commitment is demonstrated to the firm by actions not by words. Introducing a client satisfaction measurement system and using this not only to run the firm but to evaluate and reward professionals and staff is really the only effective way to actually physically demonstrate to the whole firm a real commitment to becoming market oriented.

At the root of the problems associated with developing market-oriented professional service firms is resistance to change. Given that the starting point for most professional service firms in their marketing development efforts is probably close to zero on a ten point scale, then the changes involved in becoming market oriented are enormous and

Professional culture

The whole ethos of the professions, almost by definition, creates conservation, resistance to change and even arrogance that is unsurpassed in my experience. The training, qualification and day-to-day work of professionals focuses upon technical excellence – the worst form of production orientation, and a substantial barrier to implanting and developing marketing and a market orientation.

Degree of intangibility

While most service marketers are faced by the intangible nature of service 'products', the degree of intangibility associated with many professional services is extreme. Most marketers, professionals and clients have particular problems with this issue. Few firms have yet developed convincing long-term solutions to this problem.

Customization

In most professional service marketplaces the ability of firms to standardize their service offerings and solutions is very limited. In both consumer and organizational marketplaces clients need, expect and demand that professionals use their skills, experience and expertise to demand individual customized professional service solutions for differing, individual needs. The degree of customization or 'clientization' again differentiates the professional service context from most other commercial sectors.

Client uncertainty

The level and degree of client uncertainty typically involved in the purchase of professional services is inherent in the nature of the business of professional service firms. Few marketplaces involve the lack of 'product' knowledge and associated uncertainty that is routinely found amongst clients in the professional service marketplace. It is clear that at a needs level, what clients require first and foremost is a firm that is able to reduce uncertainty and inspire client confidence.

Constantly changing legislation

Many of the professions are driven by legislation and regulation from government, professional bodies, watchdogs, etc. Professional service products are not simply developed and changed in response to client needs but also in response to changes in legislation and regulations. Few commercial sectors face the degree and rapidity of externally induced changes that is increasingly routine for professional service firms.

Involvement of staff

The inseparability of production and consumption in most professional services is extreme. The resulting level of involvement of service provision and client contact staff required in marketing is an enormous problem. While this is also true in other service sectors, in most professional service firms this results in the large majority of partners, professionals and staff being directly and explicitly involved in the firm's marketing efforts.

Partnership structure

The partnership structure of most professional service firms essentially means owner-managed businesses and management by committee. The difficulties of managing such organizational structures are enormous, not least in the areas of budgeting and the time and effort required to get firms to take concrete decisions. While partnerships are found in other commercial sectors, in no other do the vast majority of firms, and firms of such size, have partnership structures.

Individually, these characteristics of professional services and professional service firms are problematic for marketing and marketers. Collectively, they represent a unique marketing situation. These differences, and the inapplicability of research, skills and experience in marketing from other commercial sectors do constitute a strong case for consideration of professional services marketing as a discrete subject.

It is for this reason that this book, in comparison to the approaches of most others in this area, concentrates upon the specific problems faced in reality by senior managers, partners, professionals and marketers in professional services marketing and the development of market-oriented professional service firms.

This book does not represent a standard textbook. Instead it focuses upon the existing reality of marketing in the professional service context and imports from experiences, research, skills, etc. in other commercial sectors only those tools, techniques and concepts which are capable, in a highly customized way, of addressing the particular, peculiar and unique problems of professional services marketing.

While this book cannot provide professional service firms with all the answers, it does seek to enable all of those involved in professional services marketing to begin the challenge of closing the gap between what marketing has to offer the professions and what it is currently able to deliver.

Index